LOYALTY AND SACRIFICE

LOYALTY AND SACRIFICE

USHERING NEW HORIZONS

for Business Leaders in the Digital Age

RAGHU KALÉ

STRIKING**IDEAS**

Printed in the United States of America

First Printing, 2019

ISBN-13: 978-0-578-62170-8

Striking Ideas LLC
Web: *striking-ideas.com*
email: *striking-ideas.media@raghukale.com*

Dedicated to my colleagues for their extraordinary loyalty and incredible sacrifice, their selfless acts of grace and heroism in facing terror on November 26, 2008

The best way
to get something done is to begin.

— Anonymous

CONTENTS

Foreword by Ratan N Tata   *11*

Preface by Dr. Edward de Bono   *13*

Author's Note   *17*

1. The Context   **29**

 The Digital Impact   *30*

 Leading with Wisdom & Virtuous Governance   *33*

 Getting Back to Basics   *38*

2. The Human Spirit and Loyalty   **43**

 To Love is Human   *43*

 Dissecting the Definition of Loyalty   *44*

3. The Soul of Sacrifice   **51**

 Inspiring Altruism   *52*

 Selective Hearing   *54*

 Spine Chilling Accounts   *57*

 The Great Disconnect   *63*

4. Go Figure!   **67**

 Trust, Shared Values & Vision   *67*

 Beyond Quid Pro Quo   *69*

 Transactional Boundaries   *70*

 The Mistaken Identities   *72*

 The Dissonance Persists   *74*

 A New Awakening   *75*

 The L&S Principles   *79*

5. The L&S Elusive Principle   **89**

The Grand Dame of New York   *90*

The Reclusive CEO   *91*

A Lifelong Commitment   *93*

A Speeding Ticket Defines Loyalty   *95*

An Icon of Desire   *96*

For Motivation & Camaraderie   *97*

Hey, I am Loyal to My Clan   *98*

Persisting Practices Hiding in Plain Sight   *99*

6. The L&S Wallet Principle   **105**

The Doctor from London   *106*

Discerning Customers are Willing   *107*

A Collage: Reaffirming Share of Wallet   *107*

He Loved her for Life   *109*

Is That Customer Intimacy?   *109*

7. The L&S Passion Principle   **113**

I can Hear you Loud and Clear   *113*

Darn! I Dropped my Passport in a Mailbox   *114*

Living by the Company's Credo   *116*

Learning to Speed Dial   *117*

She Tracked him Down — He was Impressed   *118*

About Life Support   *120*

The Pharmacy Got Involved   *121*

Where there is No Struggle, there is No Strength   *122*

Suppressing Personal Grief   *124*

Diamonds Are Forever   *125*

Pizza Order with Toppings of Devotion   *126*

8. The L&S Silence Principle   **131**

The Reluctant Heir: Determined to Succeed   *132*

Sustaining a Thousand Year Legacy   *133*

Agency-Man Masters the Grill   *136*

A Love Hate Relationship   *138*

9. The Latency Factor   **143**

The Persisting Distortions   *143*

Learning from The Gurus   *144*

Proposing The Latency Principles   *148*

The Persistence of Hindsight-Latency   *150*

The Allure of Foresight-Latency   *151*

Mapping The Latency-Factors   *152*

Question the Unquestioned   *156*

10. The New Horizons   **161**

The Age of AI   *162*

The Shifting Demographics   *165*

Declining Trust   *167*

A Vortex of No Return   *169*

Opening Minds   *172*

Acknowledgements   *179*

List of References   *187*

Author Introduction by Raymond N Bickson   *197*

Author's Profile   *203*

Those who live in the past limit their future.

— Anonymous

Foreword by Ratan N Tata

In his book *Loyalty and Sacrifice*, Mr. Raghu Kalé emphasizes that digital progress is no longer a trend but the new norm. Artificial Intelligence and advanced algorithms are impacting lives in more ways than we are aware of, and industries are investing heavily in big data powered AI to anticipate customer needs and create hyper-personalized experiences with the intent of building customer loyalty.

These advances highlight the need to revisit old definitions of customer loyalty which can no longer be defined merely by repeat purchase. The book proposes a new definition of customer loyalty and provides all the numerous new-age factors that affect it.

It is hoped that this book will help corporates, students, and proponents of new-age businesses to understand the hidden facets of loyalty and stay relevant in an ever-changing digital age.

Ratan N Tata

Everyone is ignorant, only on different subjects.

— *Will Rogers*

This book is about loyalty and sacrifice and how they are inseparable. There are countless stories about the act of sacrifice that boldly prove one's loyalty and these two dimensions are very firmly bonded together. Unless there is a uniform definition of the basic terms and words, practical understanding and common approaches cannot be developed.

Human mind organizes information in patterns which becomes a deterrent to new ideas. The more firmly the pattern is established, the harder it becomes to dissolve the old notions. If you want to do something but feel something is preventing you, then that something is probably loyalty to some existing system — whether it is family, religion, culture, rigid bureaucratic systems thinking in corporations or anything similar. So, adherence to a particular way of thinking about things is a very crucial part of all lives.

Those of you who have read any of my books will know about my thinking on creativity and new ideas. The mind is held hostage to old ideas. This may require some courage to think and to do, but if we are to make any progress at all, then there has to be some degree of breaking from old ways; otherwise we are bound forever in old ideas.

It may also be that one of the loyalties you have to escape from is your general thinking about yourself. To understand '*sacrifice*' you also need to understand '*loyalty*' and this book helps you in both cases.

This book makes very clear what loyalty is, and its different aspects, and at the same time, reveals the hidden aspect of sacrifice, which jumps over the boundaries of loyalty.

In many of my books, particularly in *The Mechanism of Mind*, I describe how the brain controls patterns, which then control our future perception and action. The characteristic behavior of the system is shown to create and reinforce patterns. Set patterns in the system determine how new experiences are integrated. Attention tends to flow along well-worn paths and patterns have large catchment areas. Novel experiences are often lost as attention flows down old tracks that are in some way similar to the new experience. Sometimes starting at a different point in an established pattern can lead to a jump out of that pattern to a new one. These behaviors are analogs to human thinking behaviors such as circular thinking, prejudice, polarization, insight, and humor.

In a sense, any new idea is a sacrifice if it breaks the loyalty of an existing pattern. But sometimes, new ideas are necessary. We may be aware of the sacrifice involved in any particular idea and still decide whether to use it or not. And yet there are times when the sacrifice is hidden in plain sight and it gets ignored due to mental bias.

This book opens a new conversation, and I am hopeful this book will help a discussion on the hidden facets of loyalty.

Dr. Edward de Bono

It is forgivable to say nothing out of ignorance;
it's inexcusable to remain silent
once awareness dawns.

— *Joshua Ferris*

Author's Note

I t was a breezy summer evening, calm and peaceful, a perfect full moon casting its glow on the lovely golf course in the army cantonment area where I went to school during my teenage years. I was having a lively discussion with a gentleman who had served in the army. Our conversation gradually turned towards leadership in the corporate world. I was a rookie out of business school, my head full of newly acquired impressions about inspiring corporate leadership and management principles, and I was enthused about sharing my views. The colonel, meanwhile, had gone silent — I presumed he was absorbing my comments as he nursed his drink. I was not prepared for what followed.

After a long silence, he placed his drink on the table and exclaimed: *"You think you guys in the corporate world have leaders? Do you have followers who can take orders and do what is required? That really should be the key question."* He paused. I reflected. The silence was deafening. He continued: *"Knowing full well that a certain percentage of those who run across the minefield will be maimed.*

Knowing that for some, death is a certainty if they choose to run across the minefield." He paused again, I had nothing to say. The silence was a blessing. It helped me think. *"When the captain of the platoon says that we must run through a minefield and capture the post on the other side — there is no second guessing the captain. He is the first to lead and the platoon follows with zeal to achieve a tactical move — that's what leadership is all about. It takes courage. It is leading from the front — I don't see leadership in the corporate world that can match such ordeals; and yet you talk about leadership?"*

The colonel's remarks stayed with me through the years and I often pondered over our conversation. Gradually I began to grasp the elusive potential of sacrifice that is endured by all those who implicitly follow their leader. There is no time to say O captain! My captain! There is no time for grief and sorrow. In the blink of an eye the troops spring to action to execute their captain's orders. A leap of faith. An absolute trust in the leader. An alignment of shared vision and values enabling plausible action.

During my stint in hospitality, I had the good fortune to work with some of the finest hoteliers from around the world. In my endeavor to understand and unravel the mysteries and magic that create defining moments in hospitality, I had to dig deep to understand the tenets of service. How does one explain the true essence of service? A tricky question indeed.

The dictionary definition lacks depth. What made my colleagues in hotel operations enthusiastic about serving their customers? What drove them to show kindness, consideration and warmth towards strangers? On one occasion I heard this explanation: *"You can't teach people to be nice — either you have it, or you don't — some people enjoy serving others — while some are not cut out to serve."* A statement that alludes to the roots of service residing in deeper personality traits. *"Hospitality is not just a profession; it is a way of life"* — an assertion I often heard during my myriad deliberations on the subject over the years. *"The service demeanor has a cultural dimension influenced by the regions of the world — the West, the Far East, Asia, the Middle East — and religious influences emanating from cultural stands."* Everyone had something valuable to share.

On one occasion I found myself engaged in a conversation with a senior colleague, a consummate hotelier. Our chat circled around what service indeed is? This was my attempt to get to the bottom of how one truly comprehends the depth of service. Where does one draw inspiration for service? He asked me, *"...as a child do you recall ever running a fever? And then your mother taking care of you?"*

19

Promptly, I responded, *"...yes, I remember that — my mom supported and comforted me while I was sick and in pain."* Then he asked me: *"Did you thank her for the services she rendered?"* I said, *"Gosh, no! not precisely at that time!"* He pushed further, *"Did you give her a five-star rating?"* He went on and his remarks made me perceive the esoteric nature of service. That it was something spiritual. I realized that service is not about a transactional mindset — it is embedded in the very mental and attitudinal make-up of those who love to serve. Hospitality is inspired subliminally by what humanity has to offer. It can never substitute the care and affection that family bonds exude in a relationship and yet it is these human values that inspire those in the hospitality and services business and drive them to act with a passion to serve. Much like moths drawn to a flame.

Taking pleasure in serving others and drawing comfort from the smiles on their faces — this breed of people are the well-wishers and custodians of hospitality. Looking closely into the lives of my colleagues in hospitality I realize that they are truly loyal to their profession — they are ready to leap over minefields to achieve their goals and follow their passion. Extraordinary stories about frontline associates at *Taj Hotels Resorts and Palaces* going beyond the call of duty seem to be never-ending and confirm the existence of a service philosophy deeply rooted in loyalty and love for the institution. This service philosophy was conspicuous during the 2008 terror attack on the iconic Taj Hotel, Mumbai. During that tragedy, I witnessed the incredible acts of courage and selflessness of the employees of the Taj who willingly endangered their lives to save their guests and colleagues. As I listened to the poignant accounts of how the staff risked their lives, formed human walls and even took bullets to save the lives of their guests, one thing became clear — they were driven to act selflessly out of a sense of spiritual connect they felt with the hotel, a steadfast devotion to the institution and an unwavering allegiance to its ideals.

The Taj has always been known for its inimitable hospitality and the acts of its employees in extending themselves to serve guests has an unconquerable sense of duty and pride in the institution. While the world praised their courage, grace and hospitality, the Taj employees maintained that they were only doing their duty. Even in the face of imminent danger to their own lives, they continued looking after their guests — inspired by the deeply embedded values of the organization and propelled by an immense sense of loyalty towards their workplace.

And so, it appears that loyalty is the silent particle charge. It is the potential energy, an equity willing to be discharged. It is what whets the appetite to sacrifice for a cause, prompted by a clear sense of duty and desire to fulfill a mission.

Thus, loyalty and sacrifice are bonded together. These two facets are inseparable. I have witnessed closely the sacrifices of colleagues and the silent compromises that they endured. These thoughts lingered in my mind over the years and finally pushed me to write this book. The relevance of my propositions in this day and age of digital capabilities is relevant for exploring new horizons. In this book I outline my views, thoughts and propositions.

Chapter 1 – The Context

We are at the cusp of a digital revolution and it is an opportune time to take into context how the digital age is ushering change. This chapter includes a few examples that shine a spotlight on the challenges of surviving the onslaught of technology and a hope for good governance.

Chapter 2 – The Human Spirit and Loyalty

This chapter deep-dives into the facets of loyalty by citing a few anecdotes. Here, I have crafted a new definition of the word 'loyalty'. It has ramifications on sharpening a universal common definition of the term. With the accelerated pace of digital progress, it can have a long-term impact on stakeholder engagements and help design more effective employee and customer loyalty programs based on a common yardstick. This chapter proposes four fundamental loyalty axioms that apply uniformly to any human act without cherry picking.

Chapter 3 – The Soul of Sacrifice

A deep connection between the soul of sacrifice and its invisible ties to loyalty is illustrated. This deep connection is unraveled with anecdotes to amplify its relevance. Based on the foundation of loyalty axioms this chapter proposes the basic tenets of loyalty that apply to customers and employees uniformly.

CHAPTER 4 – GO FIGURE!

Go Figure! illustrates conceptually the impact of actions delivered and derived by employees and customers under a common framework. This chapter presents four *L&S Principles* of loyalty — *L&S Elusive Principle, L&S Wallet Principle, L&S Passion Principle* and *L&S Silent Principle*. A unified framework can open opportunities for a common vocabulary and facilitate a conversation to enhance the subject besides allowing measurement and identifying correlation across all four *L&S Principles*.

CHAPTER 5 – THE *L&S* ELUSIVE PRINCIPLE

Within the framework of *L&S Elusive Principle* real-life accounts illustrate the existence of sacrifice that customers endure as a mark of their loyalty. This chapter showcases a few stories and allows reflection about such occurrences that are unaccounted for in relation to measurement of loyalty in appreciation towards customers. A long lasting relationship could be secured if there was a way to unearth these blindspots. The digital revolution can trace consumer behavior in ways that was unthinkable in the past and the new age provides a platform to take into account new dimensions of loyalty that is based on the four axioms of loyalty. The real life accounts connect the dots with the new definition of loyalty.

CHAPTER 6 – THE *L&S* WALLET PRINCIPLE

Within the framework of *L&S Wallet Principle* real-life accounts illustrate consumer loyalty in accordance with a revised and unified definition that can be applied to all the stakeholders. This chapter highlights real stories that corroborate a new dimension of sacrifice as seen from the 'share of wallet' point of view.

CHAPTER 7 – THE *L&S* PASSION PRINCIPLE

When employees are passionate about their work and believe in the organization's vision and values, there is a potential for them to go beyond the call of duty to provide exceptional service to their customers. This chapter depicts the *L&S Passion Principle* through real examples of spirited employees going beyond the expected to delight their customers.

CHAPTER 8 – THE *L&S* SILENT PRINCIPLE

Sometimes the call of duty is so strong and the sense of responsibility so powerful that it drives people to make silent sacrifices for the ones they love or for the cause they believe in. This chapter showcases a few stories that illustrate this *L&S Silent Principle*.

CHAPTER 9 – THE LATENCY FACTOR

War heroes and employees sacrifice in the name of loyalty and their acts are applauded, celebrated and recognized. However, when asked if customers are capable of sacrifice it draws a blank. Customer loyalty is defined by repeat purchase which has become the basic building block to measure loyalty. Why this distortion and discrepancy in definitions? In this chapter I have attempted to explain these anomalies. This chapter dwells on heuristics and mental patterns under the umbrella of the 'Latency Factor' and defines the concepts of Hindsight Latency and Foresight Latency.

CHAPTER 10 – NEW HORIZONS

New Horizons brings out the relevance of the demographic shifts, digital capabilities, and existing practices — with a forward-looking expression to design a better tomorrow and emphasizes this as an opportune time to engage with a unified definition of 'loyalty' based on a foundation of the *L&S Principles* and puts forth a series of questions to navigate the next steps for interested audiences.

I have had the benefit of knowing professionals from myriad disciplines spread around the world who took time to read my concepts at various stages of development. During the development phase it was clear that this subject deserved a full throated expression that digs deeper into breaking mental patterns of adherence, as attention tends to flow along well-worn paths — and so this culminated in my attempt to write this book in 10 chapters for an easy read on a short flight, for corporate leaders, marketing professionals and bright minds in academia.

Indeed it is time to break away from established patterns and sharpen the definitions for ushering new horizons.

1

Round, Like a circle in a spiral
Like a wheel within a wheel
Never ending nor beginning
On an ever-spinning reel
Like a snowball down a mountain
Or a carnival balloon
Like a carousel that's turning
Running rings around the moon
Like a clock whose hands are sweeping
Past the minutes of its face
And the world is like an apple
Whirling silently in space
Like the circles that you find
In the windmills of your mind ...

— Alan Bergman and Marilyn Bergman

1. THE CONTEXT

first
things
first

The human mind's inquisitiveness and urge to discover, expand knowledge and explore the unknown has driven some of the most significant achievements in history. From the pure arts to finding solutions to complex issues, its creativity finds expression in myriad ways. Yet, the mind remains an enigma — for decades philosophers and scientists have attempted to understand what makes human beings more than just complex robots. And while the workings of the mind continue to befuddle, the field of artificial intelligence (AI) — which focuses on recreating the abilities of the human brain — has progressed stupendously and is influencing mankind in ways that we have only begun to fathom.

The Oscar-winning melody *The Windmills of Your Mind* is one of my favorite songs. Its lyrics have a somewhat allusive reference to the sentiment of holding our minds hostage to well-established thinking patterns. No wonder this melody has inspired over a hundred renditions in the past fifty years. It's a testament to this wistful melody that attracts the creative mind to these lyrics and mesmerizes listeners in its patterns. It is about familiar compliance that makes it hard to break from forceful associations.

The phenomena of holding our minds hostage to desirable patterns is not just evident in creative expression. It permeates organizations, businesses and even judicial establishments. Landmark Supreme Court judgements are cited as reference points and signal a lighthouse syndrome as precedent for other cases to follow. In the corporate world the inclination to enquire about past practice is a common occurrence when faced with conflicting or uncertain decisions. People are blinded to new ways of thinking by perspectives they acquired through past success. *The Windmills of (Y)our Mind* are all pervasive.

THE DIGITAL IMPACT

Fascinating aspects of human life are being touched by forces of digital revolution that we are only at the cusp of. Much like the way the human mind works, machines — on the basis of vast amounts of data — are becoming stunningly adept at making recommendations that influence and inform decisions we take in our daily lives. There is just no escaping from machines monitoring and analyzing our behavior. A case in point: a *Forbes* story about an angry man who went into a department store:

> *"My daughter got this in the mail!" he said. "She's still in high school, and you're sending her coupons for baby clothes and cribs? Are you trying to encourage her to get pregnant?" The manager didn't have any idea what the man was talking about. He looked at the mailer. Sure enough, it was addressed to the man's daughter and contained advertisements for maternity clothing, nursery furniture and pictures of smiling infants. The manager apologized and then called a few days later to apologize again. On the phone, though, the father was somewhat abashed. "I had a talk with my daughter," he said. "It turns out there's been some activities in my house I haven't been completely aware of. She's due in August. I owe you an apology."*[1a]

The confluence of digital technologies with decision making is churning out new realities. Bots and trolls are profoundly introducing a bias, sometimes by design, and amplifying our likes and dislikes. They are also accelerating polarization of attitudes.

The movie *Brexit* illustrates the use of digital powers to change the trajectory of a nation. Writing about the movie, the HBO website says:

> *The result of the Brexit referendum in summer 2016 caused a political earthquake ... and sent political tremors around the world. This provocative feature-length drama goes behind the scenes, revealing the personalities, strategies and feuds of the Leave and Remain campaigns. The tactics employed by Vote Leave during the data-driven campaign swayed a historically silent voting bloc that would ultimately decide the outcome of the referendum, as well as affecting future elections around the world.*

The perils of the 2016 US election is but a slow moving glacier. Andrew Keen, a British-American entrepreneur writes:

> *...rather than demonstrating the empowering glory of the Information Age — when citizens should have access to more information about candidates and issues than ever before — what we are seeing is the rise of the Misinformation Age.*[1b]

The digital revolution has hit humanity at many levels ranging from privacy — its impact on free speech and its bearing on the electoral process to the manner in which public opinion is shaped and shared on social networks, going beyond the personal sphere and influencing consumer behavior.

The Context

LEADING WITH WISDOM & VIRTUOUS GOVERNANCE

Businesses are competing on their ability to predict what a consumer is highly likely to do or want next, and the agility of delivering it, in order to optimize the customer experience and encourage loyalty in a highly competitive environment. Vast amounts of consumer data merged with refined algorithms supported by ever-improving computing power and very sophisticated measurement matrixes has enabled the development of incredibly complex algorithms that assist in reading human emotions behind nuanced and fleeting facial expressions, to maximize advertising and market research campaigns.

Specialists armed with data mining capabilities are ready to dissect with surgical precision their target audiences with an intention to modify their behavior in accordance with the goals of the masters they serve.

Are they making a Frankenstein out of us?

Are we living in an age that could best be described as — *So much data yet so little wisdom?* The so-called gurus will tell you to put your money where your mouth is. As noble as the intention behind this expression may sound, it leans towards an animal-like instinct. The digital revolution keeps putting money where its mouth is, and we know what we have got. There are respectable businesses that are not persuaded by the letter of the law alone. It takes conviction to quell temptations in conscious choices to abide by the spirit of the law and conduct their affairs by their moral compass. Even the most respected businesses can fall prey to *'seen to be doing the right thing'* rather than *'choosing to do the right thing'*. In stark comparison, tech businesses — as the new kids on the block — may lack maturity and wisdom, and yet they hold the most potent tools that can shape the future of humanity.

Issie Lapowsky is a senior writer for WIRED covering the intersection of tech, politics, and national affairs. Her article is revealing: "How Cambridge Analytica Sparked The Great Privacy Awakening":

> *On October 27, 2012, Facebook CEO Mark Zuckerberg wrote an email to his then-director of product development. For years, Facebook had allowed third-party apps to access data on their users' unwitting friends, and Zuckerberg was considering whether giving away all that information was risky. In his email, he suggested it was not: "I'm generally skeptical that there is as much data leak strategic risk as you think," he wrote at the time. "I just can't think of any instances where that data has leaked from developer to developer and caused a real issue for us."*

The Context

*... But Zuckerberg couldn't see what was right in front of him —
and neither could the rest of the world, really — until March 17,
2018, when a pink-haired whistleblower named Christopher
Wylie told The New York Times and The Guardian/Observer
about a firm called Cambridge Analytica.*

*Cambridge Analytica had purchased Facebook data on tens of
millions of Americans without their knowledge to build a
"psychological warfare tool," which it unleashed on US voters to
help elect Donald Trump as president.*

*... Wylie's words caught fire, even though much of what he said
was already a matter of public record. In 2013, two University
of Cambridge researchers published a paper explaining how they
could predict people's personalities and other sensitive details from
their freely accessible Facebook likes. These predictions, the
researchers warned, could "pose a threat to an individual's well-
being, freedom, or even life." Cambridge Analytica's predictions
were based largely on this research. Two years later, in 2015, a
Guardian writer named Harry Davies reported that Cambridge
Analytica had collected data on millions of American Facebook
users without their permission, and used their likes to create
personality profiles for the 2016 US election. However, in the heat
of the primaries, with so many polls, news stories, and tweets to
dissect, most of America paid no attention.*[1c]

The term *'digital gangsters'* seems to have been coined by the British parliament to label the leadership in the digital realm. It is no secret that companies plunder and harvest consumer data and sell it to other businesses who unlock its value by targeting consumers. *The New York Times* reported in November 2018 that *"Christopher Wylie, who helped found the voter-profiling firm, said that clothing preferences had been key to helping 'Steve Bannon build his insurgency'."*[1d]

Polarization has surely caused a wisdom deficit. An investigative piece in *The New York Times* noted:

> *Facebook has gone on the attack as one scandal after another —Russian meddling, data sharing, hate speech — has led to a congressional and consumer backlash.*

> *"We're not going to traffic in your personal life," Tim Cook, Apple's chief executive, said in an MSNBC interview. "Privacy to us is a human right. It's a civil liberty." — (Mr. Cook's criticisms infuriated Mr. Zuckerberg, who later ordered his management team to use only Android phones — arguing that the operating system had far more users than Apple's.)* [1e]

My intention is not to chime in on the argument that Tim Cook or Mark Zuckerberg appeared to be at loggerheads over; while one is passionate about protecting privacy and civil liberties, the other is ready to put their money where their mouth is. I intend to illustrate missing priorities of governance over greed.

Human progress cannot be measured solely by the yardstick of economic success — morality and ethics are important. In almost every sphere conflicting values seem to hinder progress; hence great emphasis must be placed on nurturing values that ensure holistic development.

The difference between abject criticism and constructive criticism is far too stark, yet ignored for what it can do to support progress. The lethal powers of digital technologies have been at play. A new term 'cyberbullying' has made its way into the dictionary. Vested interests use social media as their battle ground and the innocent are the victims. We are at the mercy of the wisdom of our leaders to secure practices for good governance.

In this short book, I argue that elevated awareness is required in these turbulent times to summon the better angels of our nature and fill the value based deficit that we see around us. What makes this so pressing is the relentlessly Darwinian nature of technological development. The evolutionary pressures surrounding technological growth are every bit as intense as in nature — corporations and governments are investing huge amounts of money with the intent to build faster, more effective and efficient systems, that keep consumer upgrade cycles running smoothly.

GETTING BACK TO BASICS

Typically, marketers have used consumer data to implement a system of loyalty programs that rewards purchasing behavior, in an effort to build and retain customer loyalty. These loyalty programs are used as a vehicle to drive incremental sales and grow market share. Customer loyalty has been reduced to being just a transactional relationship where repeat purchase is an indicator of customer loyalty and is rewarded with free merchandise, coupons and other incentives and the frequency of repeat purchase becomes a measure of loyalty. Somehow this makes me uneasy and forces me to go back to basics and revisit the tenets of 'loyalty' as a concept. Its origins reside in how we organize information in patterns which becomes a deterrent to new ideas. The more firmly the pattern is established, the harder it becomes to dissolve old notions. Remember *The Windmills of Your Mind?*

Practices reinforce conformance. Over time it becomes customary. Then it turns into a relevant norm. This is how definitions of certain words appear to gain contextual relevance. This book attempts to unravel the nexus between 'loyalty' and 'sacrifice'. These two human traits appear inseparable. Going beyond the call of duty is an accepted trait and seen as a dimension of sacrifice. Something that the loyal soul is willing to forgo. It is expected, accepted and celebrated. Employees and war heroes make sacrifices as they are loyal to the cause and the purpose they seem to pursue. It is clear that loyalty can't exist without sacrifice.

The question is — are customers capable of sacrifice?

There are customer loyalty programs that are central to the relationship that various brand initiatives attempt to forge with the customer. A host of studies have strived to offer insights for better decision making towards strategic goals in achieving success. And yet, the definition of loyalty as applied to employees and veterans is not the same as the definition of loyalty that is applied to customers. These distorted and skewed definitions are a result of holding the context hostage to adherence of applied norms.

The assimilation of knowledge and its application is a significant factor in considering the achievements of humanity. Digital advancements challenge us to introspect and ask ourselves what it means to be creatures of language, self-awareness and rationality.

Our best hopes of progress remain in understanding our purpose that serves not only our survival, but also our thriving; and striving to stimulate conversations and build systems that serve rather than subvert these.

This book portrays the human dimension of loyalty and sacrifice that organizations witness, celebrate, confront and sometimes, inadvertently, are oblivious to. I hope this book ignites a conversation to further the cause of humanizing our lives in these changing times.

IN SUMMARY — THE CONTEXT

★ Digital capabilities have been changing our lives. The confluence of digital technologies with decision making is churning out new realities. Bots and trolls are profoundly causing bias, sometimes by design, to amplify our likes and dislikes. Arguably it is also accelerating polarization of attitudes. The power of digital tools are used to manipulate the electorate and extract value in consumer markets and disastrous consequences of digital manipulation is threatening freedom.

★ A call for consciousness and corporate wisdom appears to be the need of the hour.

★ The marketing application of new technologies is encouraging. Convergence of the growing appetite for data and refined algorithms supported by very sophisticated measurement matrixes is mapping emotions. Dedicated effort has been put into the development of algorithms that assist in reading human emotions behind nuanced and fleeting facial expressions, to maximize advertising and market research campaigns.

2

Loyalty means nothing
unless it has at its heart
the absolute principle
of self-sacrifice.

— *Woodrow Wilson*

2. THE HUMAN SPIRIT AND LOYALTY

about
confluence
&
influence

Inseparable though it may seem, within the realm of loyalty, the core factor of sacrifice is silently concealed. The fallen soldiers of our many wars hold testimony to the ultimate sacrifice in their commitment to the nation. The surviving veterans of the great world wars of the past century know in their hearts the soul of sacrifice and what loyalty truly means.

TO LOVE IS HUMAN

The stories of the many war heroes who perished, and the scarred experiences of the numerous who survived, tied by a common bond of loyalty and silent sacrifices they endured, are unfathomable for others. At a human level, *The Gift of the Magi*, a famous short story by O. Henry illustrates all that one can relate to about love, loyalty, and sacrifice.

One dollar and eighty-seven cents. That was all that she had managed to save for Christmas. It was not enough for a present for him. She had planned on getting something fine and rare for her husband. Of course they had each other. But if there was any possession that they treasured most, it was the two things they owned. One was his gold watch. It had once belonged to his great-grandfather. The other was her beautiful, brown hair which was more precious than any queen's jewels. Both get a stunning surprise on Christmas Eve. She sells her hair to buy him a silver chain for his wristwatch, while he has sold his wristwatch to buy her the combs that she had seen in a shop window and desired for a long time.[2a]

Brands are made up of emotions and many factors beyond mere terms of materialism. Where are such nuggets of sacrifice that silently affirm loyalty?

DISSECTING THE DEFINITION OF LOYALTY

The *Financial Times Lexicon* defines 'customer loyalty' as: *"Customer loyalty can be said to have occurred if people choose to use a particular shop or buy one particular product, rather than use other shops or buy products made by other companies."*[2b] However, this old school definition of 'customer loyalty' appears shallow and inadequate as it ignores the facets of unwavering devotion and unconditional dedication that some customers may have for the brand.

It makes sense to pause and reflect on what author and writer Jorge Luis Borges rightly said: *"It is often forgotten that dictionaries are artificial repositories, put together well after the languages they define. The roots of language are irrational and of a magical nature."*

Word meanings expand, evolve and alter over time, influenced by social, political, religious, economic and technological forces. Hence, there's a need to shine some new light on the true tenets of loyalty. Loyalty is a lens through which humans see the world around them to make a judgment about their willingness to accommodate, to adjust, perhaps even to sacrifice. Despite differences, having an appetite for compromise and cooperation. The essence of willing to accommodate, compromise and cooperate is the (self) sacrifice quotient.

To ensure a unified understanding of the word 'loyalty', I have attempted, first, to offer my own definition of it and also referenced its word origin dating back to *circa*~1400.[2c]

LOYALTY (N.) | *ˈloiəltē* |

Loyalty: A human trait about willingness to *accommodate* or *adjust*. Despite differences willing to *compromise* and *cooperate* due to believing in the cause. A confluence of *shared values* and *shared vision* giving rise to a *tendency to accommodate*. Though strongmen demand loyalty it can only occur with the highest *alignment of shared values and vision*. Stronger alignment of *shared values* and *vision* can result in *self-sacrifice* and weaker alignment results in *willingness to go beyond the call of duty, adapt, (silently) compromise* and *cooperate*. Sometimes acts of loyalty are *silent*.

Word Origin: *c. 1400, from Old French loialte, leaute "loyalty, fidelity; legitimacy; honesty; good quality" (Modern French loyauté), from loial (see loyal). The Medieval Latin word was legalitas. The earlier Middle English form was leaute (mid-13c.), from the older French form. Loyalty oath first attested in 1852.* Allegiance: *is a matter of principle, and applies especially to conduct; the oath of allegiance covers conduct only.* Loyalty: *is a matter of both principle and sentiment, conduct and feeling; it implies enthusiasm and devotion* [Century Dictionary, 1897].

A holistic view about what loyalty means deserves four fundamental axioms.

1. **LOYALTY AXIOM OF SILENCE**
   It is never about being in the spotlight.

2. **LOYALTY AXIOM OF LATITUDE**
   Spanning a range of traits from self-sacrifice on one extreme to willingness to adjust, compromise or accommodate.

3. **LOYALTY AXIOM OF SHARED VALUES AND VISION**
   Illuminates in a confluence of shared values and shared vision — propelled to go beyond the call of duty.

4. **LOYALTY AXIOM OF FUTILITY**
   Demanding loyalty is an act in futility. It can only occur with the highest alignment of shared values and vision.

Across millennia, countless tales illustrate silent sacrifice in the name of loyalty. A steadfast devotion to loved ones. Uncompromising loyalty forged by firm beliefs that embrace human emotions.

You don't earn loyalty in a day.
You earn loyalty day-by-day.
— Jeffrey Gitomer

Greater love hath no man than this,
that a man lay down his life for his friends.
— A verse from the Bible | John 15:13

The important thing is this: To be able, at any moment, to sacrifice
what we are for what we could become...
— Maharishi Mahesh Yogi

Loyalty to an unjust cause is a perversion of honor.
— Brian Herbert

IN SUMMARY — HUMAN SPIRIT AND LOYALTY

★ Loyalty is a human trait and has been around from the time of human existence. Within the realm of loyalty, the core factor of sacrifice is silently concealed and is inseparable. Across millennia, countless tales illustrate silent sacrifice in the name of loyalty.

★ Word meanings expand, evolve and alter over time, influenced by various forces. The old school definition of 'customer loyalty' appears shallow and inadequate as it ignores the unwavering devotion that some customers may have for the brand. Hence, there's a need to shine some new light on the true tenets of loyalty.

★ Loyalty is a lens through which humans see the world around them to make a judgment about their willingness to accommodate, to adjust, perhaps even to sacrifice. Despite differences, having an appetite for compromise and cooperation.

★ A holistic view of what loyalty truly means can be understood by four fundamental axioms.

3

A deep distress has humanised my soul.

— *William Wordsworth*

3. THE SOUL OF SACRIFICE

reflective
recall of
real-life
incidents

He died on March 8, 1935, at the age of 11. After 76 years, scientists finally concluded the cause of his death — terminal cancer and a filaria infection. The report also identified four yakitori skewers in his stomach, but the skewers did not damage his stomach or cause his death. I am talking about Hachikō the Japanese Akita. Even today the dog is revered for his dedication and loyalty. For nine years, nine months and fifteen days, until the day he died, Hachikō waited at the Shibuya train station for his owner, Professor Hidesaburō Ueno, an agricultural scientist who suffered a cerebral hemorrhage while giving a lecture, and died without ever returning to the train station where Hachikō waited everyday at the precise time when the train the professor regularly took, was scheduled to arrive.

INSPIRING ALTRUISM

The life of another being is not less relevant. Life is precious no matter what form it takes. Empathy is rarely on display but it is rooted in the spirit and not shy of being exposed in a genuine heart. Richard Gere said that he cried like a baby as he read the script of the movie, *Hatchi*, a moving remake based on Hachikō's life.

In the summer of 1934, a bronze statue of Hachikō was installed at the Shibuya Station in Japan. Hachikō was present at the unveiling of the sculpture and died the following year, alone, on the street near the station. During world war II, the bronze statue was recycled due to scant resources running the nation dry. Barely 100 weeks after the world war ended, devastating humanity with the long-term effects of the mushroom cloud that loomed over Japan, the Japanese authorities and citizens did not fail to remember Hachikō. Once again in 1948, a new statue of Hachikō was erected and unveiled. It is now a typical starting point for anyone visiting Shibuya and the bronze statue is a tourist attraction.

Dogs are the best barometers of humanity. An international team of researchers points out in *The Scientist* that dogs might have been domesticated as far back as 32,000 years ago.

Why does it take a dog to bring out the best in mankind?
Is it because dog spelt backward is just an expression in disguise?

Dog tales never end. In a rare case of faithfulness, a Doberman in Bhubaneswar, India fought a bloody battle with four mountain cobras and killed all of them and later lost its life due to snake bites while guarding the home entrance. The national newspaper reported an emotional account from the dog's owner: *"I'm shocked. He has made the supreme sacrifice for me and my family. I will remember him till our death. I pray to God — May his soul rest in peace."*[3a]

The PDSA Dickin Medal is the highest award any animal can receive whilst serving in military conflict. It is recognized worldwide as the animals' Victoria Cross. Instituted in 1943 it acknowledges outstanding acts of bravery or devotion to duty displayed by animals serving with the Armed Forces or Civil Defence units in any theatre of war throughout the world. In their roll of honor appears Gander:

> *For saving the lives of Canadian infantrymen during the Battle of Lye Mun on Hong Kong Island in December 1941. On three documented occasions Gander, the Newfoundland mascot of the Royal Rifles of Canada engaged the enemy as his regiment joined the Winnipeg Grenadiers, members of Battalion*

Headquarters 'C' Force and other Commonwealth troops in their courageous defence of the Island. Twice Gander's attacks halted the enemy's advance and protected groups of wounded soldiers. In a final act of bravery the war dog was killed in action gathering a grenade. Without Gander's intervention many more lives would have been lost in the assault.

Loyalty appears to show itself beyond the human species and is a divine character of intelligent life form and its presence ought not to be ignored. The military has dedicated memorials recognizing and honoring the heroism and loyalty of war dogs that have served in various conflicts.

SELECTIVE HEARING

What baffles me is that while business enterprises are quick to adopt principles of military strategy in the organization, they ignore the parameters of loyalty and sacrifice in the realms of customers and employees. Sounds like a case of selective hearing and lack of attention.

In the last century, the business world has plundered concepts from military strategy and adapted them in their organizations. The principles prescribed by Sun Tzu (孫子), the Chinese general and army strategist (c. 5th century BC) in his ancient military treatise *The Art of War*, have been liberally borrowed by business gurus. More recently, Army Lt. Gen. H.R. McMaster, spoke on the subject: "What businesses can learn from the military"[3b] at the Kellogg On Growth forum. In his address he used examples from recent military history to provide lessons for companies.

Undoubtedly, many leadership principles and learnings from the code of military culture comfortably apply to business organizations. Just as the military honors soldiers and recognizes their acts of supreme courage in the line of fire, organizations recognize and reward employees that go beyond the call of duty. Like soldiers devoted to their country and its cause proudly carry out their duties, there are many employees who passionately believe in the cause they serve, and are loyal to their profession and their responsibilities. They do it for the love of it, not to be in the spotlight.

The truly driven, certainly don't do it just for winning recognition. And so, an interplay of loyalty and silent sacrifice is evident. If someone is intensely loyal, then there lurks the potential for them to endure sacrifice. But while business organizations attempt to 'learn' from the military, the correlation of loyalty and sacrifice, which is loudly applauded in the military, is rendered silent in the context of 'customer loyalty'.

Bill Murphy Jr., contributing editor at *inc.com* writes: *"In honor of the Army's 239th birthday, here are some of the top leadership lessons I learned from serving in and reporting on the United States Army."* In his article, he writes about "23 Things Great Leaders Always Do". The list of 23 is impressive and ranges from the need to identify clear objectives, gather intelligence, plan a course for action, stepping to the front and so on. One caught my attention:

> *"Sacrifice as necessary — When it's cold or wet or dangerous, soldiers want to know that their leader isn't asking them to do anything he or she won't do himself or herself. This is a universal leadership principle. If you're telling your team members that they have to work weekends or tightening your department's budget, you'd better be willing to share the pain.* [3c]

The factors of sacrifice are far more significant in the military and even in business. It is undoubtedly far beyond working weekends and tightening budgets.

The Soul of Sacrifice

SPINE CHILLING ACCOUNTS

In contrast to delusions of self-imposed importance of corporate leaders, I am reminded of a spine chilling true story of what civilians can do for military success.

With the war clouds looming it was time for some unusual human behavior born out of necessity, manifesting in a display of loyalty and silent sacrifice. The raw courage of a young girl propelled her to operate as an undercover agent. Her actions saved thousands of lives during the war and helped her country to victory. Her father was a diehard patriot who maintained extensive trade links with the enemy country and worked as an undercover agent. Faced with cancer, he realized time was not on his side. Urgency dictated that he should find someone who he could blindly trust. His only daughter took on the baton. Exuding his influence the father was able to get his daughter married off to the son of a high-ranking officer in the armed forces of the enemy country. In spite of being in love with someone else, she agreed to the alliance, a choice that was probably influenced by her patriotic upbringing. This marriage placed her as an undercover spy in close proximity to powerful forces in the enemy country. Having won her in-laws' confidence, she rapidly infiltrated the inner circle. She also began teaching at the local military school where children and

57

grandchildren of army top brass attended school. Her strategy and influence helped her father-in-law gain spotlight, moving her closer to the inner circle.

Though she was meant to be just a facilitator, and to observe and listen, she went a step ahead to gather critical classified information about the enemy's plans of attack. It speaks volumes about her initiative, courage, guts and risk-taking capabilities. She passed on crucial information about enemy positions, troop movements, strike plans and blueprints across the border. The intelligence she passed on helped thwart a devastating attack on the naval fleet of her motherland and destroyed the enemy capability. This information was a core factor in ending the war.

In pursuit of her mission, she had to cold-bloodedly kill her brother-in-law and the loyal manservant of her husband's household. These traumatic choices that she was forced to make, affected her deeply. Eventually, when her cover got compromised, she was rescued in a state of deep depression and pregnant with the child of her husband who she had to abandon.

It took many years for her to return to a life of normalcy. Although her father had left her his estate, she chose to settle down in a remote village. She lived like a recluse, in complete anonymity. She gave up her son because she was carrying the guilt of being a murderer, of killing other's children. She became profoundly spiritual and remained detached in her relationships. Her only unwavering attachment and loyalty remained towards her motherland and wherever she lived, the national flag would fly over her roof, till she passed away.[3d]

What explains the feeling that pushes people to endanger their own lives for another person or cause? When a renowned luxury hotel in Mumbai was under siege, its employees formed a human shield to evacuate guests to safety. In spite of knowing all the back exits and pathways through the hotel, they chose to stay back and look after their guests. Even after a decade this extraordinary behavior perplexes many. *"Why did the employees stay at their posts, jeopardizing their safety in order to save hotel guests?"* It has become the subject of a Harvard case study and continues to intrigue students as they analyze the case as part of their learning engagement:

On November 26, 2008, heavily armed terrorists launched a series of attacks throughout the western-Indian city of Mumbai (formerly Bombay). One of the locations attacked was the Taj Mahal Palace and Tower, which was occupied by the terrorists for over three days, resulting in the deaths of 34 people and 28 people injured. However, the Taj received praise in the aftermath of the attacks for the selfless actions of the staff in placing the safety of the hotel's guests before their own and working to save the lives of its guests. This case seeks to address how leaders develop a customer-centric organization, as well as how an organization saves its flagship brand after a crisis. [3c]

The soul connects to earthly realities — rooted in a deep belief of serving a cause. It is incomprehensible how even death becomes inconsequential when going beyond the call of duty.

In September 1941, when German forces began their siege of Leningrad, choking food supply to the city's two million residents, one group of people preferred to starve to death despite having plenty of 'food'. As the invading Germans poured into the city, scientists and workers at the Institute of Plant Industry barricaded themselves inside their vaults. They weren't trying to save their lives but rather the future of humanity. For, they had the unenviable task of protecting the greatest collection of seeds and tubers in the world from both hungry Soviet citizens and the rampaging German Army, for future generations.

As the siege dragged out for 900 days, one by one these heroic men started dying of hunger. And yet not one of them touched the treasure trove of seeds they were guarding — literally with their lives. They chose to starve to death despite sitting on huge supplies of potatoes, rice and other food staples.

Alexander Stchukin, the man in charge of groundnut supplies, was found dead slumped over his desk. Just a few days later, his colleague Dmitry Ivanov who was the head of the Institute's rice collection, also died. In the end, the Institute survived the war. After almost three years of horror, the supplies remained intact and all accounted for.

And so, was the sacrifice made by Stchukin, Ivanov and the other scientists worth it? Undoubtedly. Even today, farmers around the world — including in the United States — grow crops that have been developed from the genetically-modified seeds of the Vavilov Institute of Plant Industry. Modern-day scientists have cross-bred crop varieties with the varieties the brave Russians guarded with their lives to produce plants that can resist extreme temperatures and all kinds of pests. [3f]

When purpose and values are in alignment no barrier can withstand an act of loyalty.

On December 26, 1944, 29 year-old First Lieutenant John Robert Fox deliberately called for artillery fire on his own position during World War II in order to defeat a German attack in Italy, as his position had been overrun by the enemy.

The mountain village of Sommocolonia in Italy had been overrun by Germans, and Americans were in retreat. A few Americans volunteered to remain behind, however. Fox, who was an artillery spotter, was one of them. He was the "eyes" of artillery units miles from Sommocolonia. His job was to radio the coordinates that told the units where to deliver their payloads.

Fox volunteered to remain behind in order to direct defensive fire to provide cover for retreating soldiers. He found a house to hide in and, from the second floor, he used his radio to contact his colleagues. He called for artillery fire to be directed at the village in order to give the US forces time to retreat, regroup and then launch a counter-attack. Fox even specifically ordered a barrage of fire on his exact position. The gunner who received the message pointed this out to him, assuming it must be some mistake. Fox, however, simply said: "Fire it. There's more of them than there are us".

Fox's act of heroism gave his comrades the chance to regroup and launch a successful counterattack. When the US army entered Sommocolinia, they found Fox's body surrounded by the bodies of around 100 Germans. Fox had plenty of time to escape. In fact, senior officers expected Fox and the other members of his unit to abandon the village when it became clear that the Germans would overrun it. But he stayed and made the ultimate sacrifice of his life.[3g]

Skeptics may view these incidents as extremes. Out of the ordinary. However, these are tendencies that exist, and such a trajectory persists in human endeavor. When under a perfect alignment of shared values and shared vision there is a total and complete eclipse, all that beams out is a light that shines upon pure loyalty. There exists a natural appetite in humans *(as well as animals)* to act in selfless ways, to allow accommodations, and to accept.

THE GREAT DISCONNECT

In the case of employees, the term 'loyalty' is in perfect congruence when used for those who silently go beyond the call of duty and sacrifice something. But when it comes to customers, a string of repeat purchases and regular store visits is considered the bare minimum requirement to shower the label of loyalty upon them. A disconnect indeed.

Call *it* what you want — sacrifice, compromise, willing to let go, forgive and forgo. These are woven into a *string* of tendencies from extreme to the not so intense, and it is still a range that displays a quotient of sacrifice within the realm of loyalty. This *string* is the qualifying mark for loyalty. Somehow repeat purchase is not a surrogate that can earn a seat at the loyalty table.

There are two facets of loyalty. An act of loyalty is never triggered to seek attention; yet it may put the loyal soul under spotlight. On the other hand there are some silent acts of loyalty that are kept covert and concealed from public knowledge and remain unacknowledged.

> *Repeat business or behavior can be bribed.*
> *Loyalty has to be earned.*
> — Janet Robinson

> *Loyalty is a continuous phenomenon,*
> *you don't score points for past action.*
> — Natasha Pulley

In Summary — The Soul of Sacrifice

★ This chapter cites several real anecdotes that demonstrate the inseparable nature of sacrifice that is the kernel of loyalty.

★ It is concluded that shades of sacrifice reside in a range that are woven into a string of tendencies from extreme to the not so intense, and it is still a latitude that displays a quotient of sacrifice within the realm of loyalty. This string is the qualifying mark for loyalty. Somehow repeat purchase is not a surrogate that can earn a seat at the loyalty table.

★ Many leadership principles and learnings from the code of military culture comfortably apply to business organizations. Military honors soldiers and recognizes their acts of supreme courage in the line of fire, organizations recognize and reward employees that go beyond the call of duty. But while business organizations attempt to 'learn' from the military, the correlation of loyalty and sacrifice — which is loudly applauded in the military — is rendered silent in the context of 'customer loyalty'. It begs the question: *can customers be truly capable of sacrifice?*

4

*If you're not confused,
you're not paying attention.*

—Tom Peters

4. GO FIGURE!

Relationships blossom when one enhances the value of the other without directly demanding a *quid pro quo*. The only way a relationship will last is if you are inclined to give more than you are willing to take.

The central principle in any relationship is the reciprocal spirit of giving one's best for the other. A journey of constant renewal. Trials and tribulations. Learning to forgive and forgo. A state of perpetual evolution. An unwavering trust. This is universal to any relationship between spouses, siblings, families, clans or brands.

TRUST, SHARED VALUES & VISION

If a bond of sacred trusts exists, people willingly take risks and go beyond the call of duty. What sets the Navy SEAL teams apart is not just their *IQ* and the training rigor that they are subjected to, but also a very silent and yet, the most potent ingredient of all — Trust. A code of unquestionable confidence and trust holds the Navy SEALs together. A foundation that's perhaps the single most relevant factor of all. Such is the case in human to human interactions and also between business entities and people. How people respond to corporate brands and branded products is also fascinating. To some it's mind boggling that there are people who have such great attachment to inanimate objects and entities that it triggers a certain sensation in them. A certain emotion. In fact, there's a field of study dedicated to unraveling this mystery. The single-minded devotion of some people towards their preferred brands and the craze to possess newer versions of their favorite products is as real as it can get.

It is widely accepted in the business arena that being able to convert customer complaints to customer delight is a valuable asset. This may sound counter intuitive but numerous studies and practices have demonstrated that negativity of complaints is transformed into positive experiences, on resolution. Customer complaints are good for business, someone said. But then, one can't go around causing problems to instigate an array of irate customers just to create an opportunity to start solving customer complaints. Those engaged on the frontline to resolve complaints, don't operate with a mindset of *quid pro quo*. Their priority is to see how they can give their best to resolve the grievance. The genuineness and sincerity of their approach is all that matters. And this is what happens in the real world. Emotions are at play. Resolutions are reached. Forgive and forgo is amicable. There is an unseen set of values in alignment between those served (*customers*) and those serving (*frontline*) and a silent hope for the future.

These are shared values and shared vision in a sublime state. When customers appreciate and embrace a business enterprise's values and vision, and trust it to deliver on its promises, it turns into shared values and shared vision. The conflux of such recipes lays out a banquet to celebrate progress for humanity — and everyone is invited.

BEYOND QUID PRO QUO

Solving customer complaints without expecting *quid pro quo* and getting the job done fulfills a noble intent. Employees engaged in solving a problem most often have their minds genuinely absorbed in fixing the problem. In most cases, their real concern is to serve the customer. These are the defining moments for the customer. That is what they will remember.

And this is what they will narrate. These are elusive and nebulous thoughts that escape systems thinking.

Having a transactional mindset has its relevance and yet the spirit of engagement beyond mere transactions has a very significant place in deciding what is relevant. This is best understood by referring to the early stages that set the foundation of the civil code in human civilization. True justice is not always evident in abiding by transactional ways. Following the *lex talionis code* of *'an eye for an eye and a tooth for a tooth'* as it prevailed in primitive, tribal societies is irrelevant today. If the *lex talionis code* were pursued today it would render many blind and many others signing a contract with the tooth fairy. However, the *lex talionis code* has its relevance in the conceptual makeup. The modern day legal system has evolved and is more complex in arriving at what is just and fair. The broader point here is that the transactional framework has its relevance.

TRANSACTIONAL BOUNDARIES

Hindsight thinking to justify a proposition is not difficult to find. The difference between desire and decision is that the former is an intent absorbed by an overwhelming range of factors, while the latter is an outcome of a final judgement in sealing all options in favor of a final choice. There is more to life than mere transactions. However, the tenets of transactions are relevant to revere the boundaries they serve.

It is generally assumed that customers are rational. Transactionally speaking, customers pay a price because they expect value in return and the difference between the value they get and the price they pay is the derived benefit.

A Gartner Study titled "Customer Loyalty Myths Debunked" states:

> *Many companies try to drive customer loyalty by delighting customers — exceeding their expectations with above-and-beyond service. Yet this strategy is difficult and costly to deliver. Worse, it fails to provide a proportional increase in loyalty.*[4a]

There is a realization about the perils of the inadequacy of the definition of 'loyalty' as illustrated in a comment on a Gartner blog:

> *The problem with many loyalty programs is that they don't actually deliver loyalty. They deliver repeat purchases, and repeat purchases may look a lot like loyalty, but you cannot know what is driving preference and purchases unless you listen to and understand customer perception. A good loyalty program can*

produce ROI by delivering incremental revenue in excess of program costs, but brands must never mistake loyalty to their points and incentives with genuine loyalty to their brand.[4b]

The stronger the pattern of associating customer loyalty with repeat purchase the more distorted the meaning of the word 'loyalty' becomes.

How did we get such a pretty distorted definition of loyalty?

THE MISTAKEN IDENTITIES

Before we attempt to unravel the mystery surrounding loyalty, here is a short incident worth pondering over that involved my wife and my three daughters.

When we moved to our new home on Arthur Street my daughters aged 9, 12 and 14 spotted a mouse as we decided to have a late night ice cream treat from the game room. Oooh! she cried out loud seeing the mouse at the corner of the floor cabinet. Their eyes met, and he decided to jump in the most unexpected direction to escape. Courageous, I recall thinking, how brave of the mouse to make that jump. But alas he was attempting to scoot and nothing more. Then next week it happened again; my dear wife spotted the adorable pink happy fellow running across the kitchen. We have another sighting, I said. This guy knows his way. He is a repeat visitor. The breaking news was made at the breakfast table next morning. My wife narrated her experience, and my daughters chimed in about their encounter with the mouse: how their eyes met and how brave this handsome pink champion was. By then my daughters had already named this guy as Jaq. I recall reacting — Whoa! Don't honor this guy with a name. He is not your pet. He has done nothing for you other than regularly visiting to serve his own cause. He is a bargain hunter. He is here to fill his belly. He is not here for you. He is here for himself. This happened again after a fortnight. This time it was a pair of mice sprinting across the kitchen. By now my daughters had named the companion too. The duo was called Jaq and Gus. Once the garbage bin was removed and the doors sealed it was time for no love lost. Perhaps they cared nothing more than just fulfilling their own desires and we never saw them again. Perhaps they found a better opportunity in life.

Now is there a parallel with repeat visitors who visit only to serve their cause? Don't be fooled even if they visit multiple times; we recognize they were not there because they were in love with you. They were there for their own selfish needs. Labeling such people with an over used phrase like 'customer loyalty' is no more than a case of mistaken identity. Beware next time you hear or use the term 'customer loyalty'. Pause and think — if there exists any tone of reverence in the word you just chose to use. It is unfair to some real diehard customers who truly are loyal.

Loyalty can't be explained in shallow terms of repeat purchase but as a robust cause and effect between value proposition, price paid and benefit derived. These dimensions are quantifiable and a framework such as this can be the basis of measuring customer loyalty in a scientific way rather than relying on heuristics or assumptions about surrogate measures of repeat purchase.

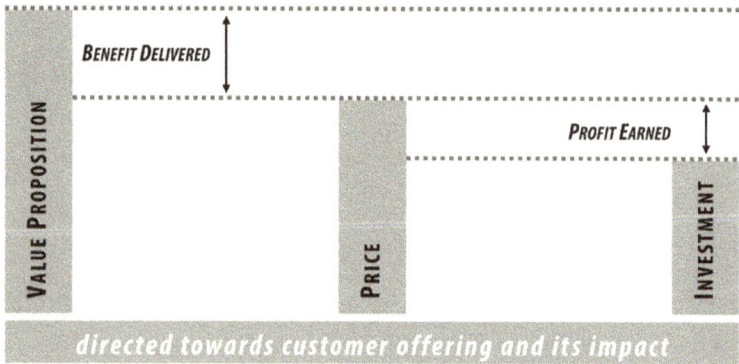

THE DISSONANCE PERSISTS

Ever since the dawn of humanity, to present-day commerce, there is one thing in common. An exchange was and will always be at the heart of trade and business. Even in the days of the barter, consumers expected something of higher value in exchange.

A *Forbes* article paints a grim picture about how grossly the existing definition of customer loyalty lacks credibility:

> *Customer loyalty isn't what it used to be. In fact, research company Access Development reported that 79% of customers would take their business to a competitor within a week of experiencing poor customer service, while the estimated cost of customers switching their choice of businesses due to poor service is $1.6 trillion. Keeping this in mind, how can businesses strengthen their customer loyalty in a world where customer sentiment is constantly shifting and consumers have more options than ever before of where to spend their money?* [4c]

Why should one continue to invest in a failed definition of customer loyalty that is no longer relevant?

A NEW AWAKENING

It is time to craft a new definition of customer loyalty. One that is not riddled with a regimented view of how to create loyalty based on repeat purchase patterns.

The skewed old definition of 'customer loyalty', as widely understood and accepted, is symptomatic of fettered thinking. Let's take a relook at the popular definition of 'customer loyalty' that I had shared earlier in chapter 2:

FINANCIAL TIMES — *ft.com/lexicon*
DEFINITION OF CUSTOMER LOYALTY

> *Customer loyalty can be said to have occurred if people choose to use a particular shop or buy one particular product, rather than use other shops or buy products made by other companies.*

> *Customer loyalty is the key objective of customer relationship management and describes the loyalty which is established between a customer and companies, persons, products or brands.*

> *The individual market segments should be targeted in terms of developing customer loyalty.*

In chapter 2, I have also outlined the four axioms of loyalty. The *Loyalty Axiom of Futility* states that demanding loyalty is an act in futility. Loyalty can only occur with the highest alignment of shared values and vision. Inducing conveniences to encourage repeat purchase is akin to demanding loyalty and this is at the heart of the failed definition of loyalty. We need a definition that is not simply based on what the customer gets out of the emotional connect that the product or service creates — it is not just about what the customer gains from the transaction that determines the relationship but is rather an equation of what or how much the customer is willing to accommodate, forgo, accept, and tolerate, for a product or service. Such a definition requires a more accommodating outlook that includes all the four axioms of loyalty covered in chapter 2.

This new definition will take into account the nature of loyalty and its extent — which is a holistic view of customer loyalty — and the forces that drive loyalty, and the intensity of its manifestation.

PRESENTING THE NEW
L&S CUSTOMER LOYALTY DEFINITION

Customer loyalty can be said to have occurred when customers have a willingness to accommodate and make concessions. The manifestation of such accommodation resides in the confidence that customers have in the product, corporate or the brand towards which the loyalty occurs. As the very nature of loyalty is not about attracting attention or to be in the spotlight, the acts of loyalty can range from being elusive to willing to sacrifice one's share of wallet.

The intensity of loyalty is directly correlated to the level of attachment to shared values and shared vision that customers feel affinity to. Brand platforms provide elements for such engagements.

Demanding loyalty is an act in futility. It can only occur with the highest alignment of shared values and vision. Customer Loyalty cannot be attracted by way of surrogate measure of repeat purchase as such enticement evokes the Loyalty Axiom of Futility.

Without a mindset of giving, that is reciprocal on both sides, and a means of appreciating such a gesture acknowledged with a measurement matrix and backed by a sense of gratitude, genuine, loyal relationship is just an aspiration.

Identifying relevant drivers — as enumerated in the four Loyalty Axioms and taking cognizance of what makes the customer willing to give in to and willing to accommodate, is critical. When such drivers are nurtured over time, it can result in a change in the repeat purchase behavior of consumers and their preferences for a brand.

Go Figure!

What is the nature of customer loyalty
that is reciprocal and the foundation to relationship building?

The answer lies somewhere in shared values. Relationships based on a firm foundation of shared values and a longterm view of a shared vision; and an inner potential to forgive and forgo and exceed an expected threshold. Countless examples of product recall demonstrate an appetite for loyal deeds as customers seem to be forgiving and strong brands sustain in the long run on the strength of shared values. Loyal investors play long-term bets, and short-term earnings per share are endured for the sake of a long-term shared vision.

There are numerous deeds that hold testimony to loyalty to the cause, loyalty to the purpose, loyalty to the clan, family, friends, company, brand, customer, colleagues and an array of everything that is relationship worthy.

THE L&S PRINCIPLES

Inspired by the silent accommodations of elusive customers and their striking generosity and the passion and perseverance of employees quietly contributing beyond the call of duty, without expecting any reward in return, I have crafted the four tenets of *L&S Principles*.

Two of the four tenets are customer facing — *L&S Elusive Principle* and *L&S Wallet Principle*.

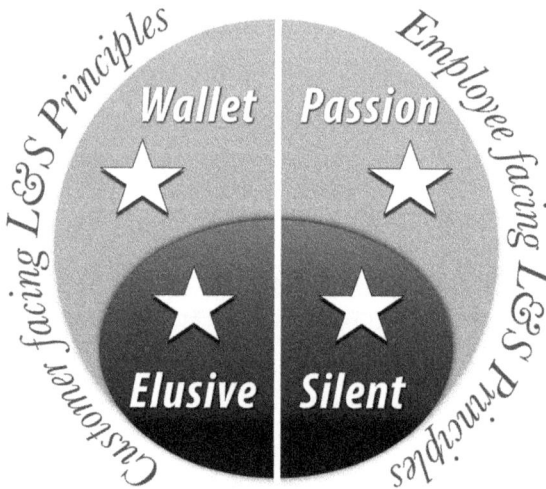

Real life anecdotes underline the sentiments of the *L&S Elusive Principle* in chapter 5. The generosity of customers and their willingness to sacrifice the share of wallet is captured in true stories in chapter 6 that highlight the *L&S Wallet Principle*.

The other two tenets are employee facing — *L&S Passion Principle* illustrated through heartwarming stories of employees exceeding expectations in chapter 7 and *L&S Silent Principle* demonstrated through real life anecdotes in chapter 8 about the silent contributions of employees devoted to their work.

THE *L&S* ELUSIVE PRINCIPLE

At the heart of the L&S Elusive Principle lies the first Loyalty Axiom of Silence that will always be central to a customer's decision making. It is never about being in the spotlight. The second is the Loyalty Axiom of Latitude that is about the level of endurance and accommodation customers are willing to accept which is again linked to the third Loyalty Axiom of Shared Values and Vision. All three axioms are inter related.

Profit is the difference between price and all costs and investments. That's the essence of business. Paying a price and expecting something more valuable in return as derived benefit makes it an interesting dynamic.

A change in price impacts profitability and impacts the perception about benefit derived from the promised value

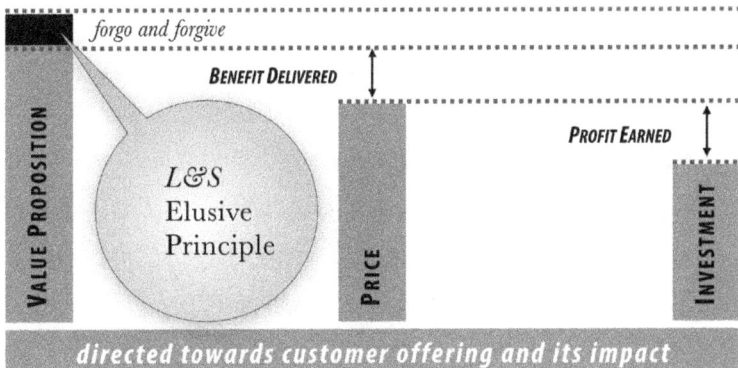

proposition. Hidden therein, in everything that is directed towards customer offering — and its impact — are two primary ways in which customers sacrifice in earnest. Ways that have been unexplained so far.

Even as consumerism permeates the world, its vocabulary remains shallow and often misses appropriate nomenclatures that define such actions. The terms *Loyalty Programs* and *Rewards Programs* are often interchangeably used. Some attempt to differentiate one from the other by spotting transactional parameters such as short-term cashing out a payback in rewards programs while loyalty programs tend to draw out, luring customers to hang in there in the hope of a long-term benefit and to be part of an elite clan.

THE *L&S* WALLET PRINCIPLE

At the heart of the L&S Wallet Principle resides the Loyalty Axiom of Futility. Loyalty cannot be demanded and therefore enticing repeat purchase will not yield loyal customers as it is an act in futility. The Loyalty Axiom of Latitude will dictate the level of price inelasticity that is endured by the customer that is directly proportional to the Loyalty Axiom of Shared Values and Vision.

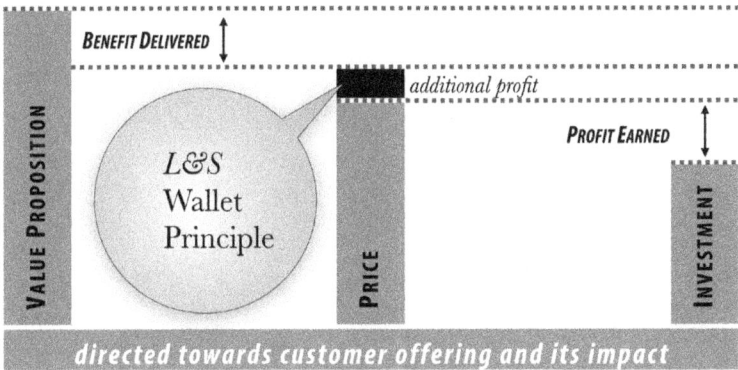

The foundation for a longterm relationship resides in the L&S Wallet Principle as value is measured over a lifetime and lifecycle of brands.

Many scholarly papers have been exploring the empirical relationship between loyalty and price elasticity in purchase behavior and argue that loyal consumers will be less price sensitive. Measuring elasticity to assess loyalty is a far more pertinent measure than repeat purchase. Therefore, the *L&S Wallet Principle* has its relevance in price inelasticity.

And what about employees? They invest their time and put a higher effort in carrying out their duties and responsibilities — while drawing remuneration for their efforts — thereby providing a value proposition that exceeds in perception and making an impact on customers. A higher effort will almost instantly result in higher investment from the employees' side thereby making an impact for the customer. The correlation of these three variables have an agile demeanor.

THE *L&S* PASSION PRINCIPLE

The core building block that defines the organizational culture is central to L&S Passion Principle that is anchored in the Loyalty Axiom of Shared Values and Vision. How the employees perceive the organizational purpose reflects their external posture.

In fact, there are studies that suggest that a high level of emotional connect with one's organizational values drives up discretionary effort on the part of an employee which in turn increases the customer perceived value.

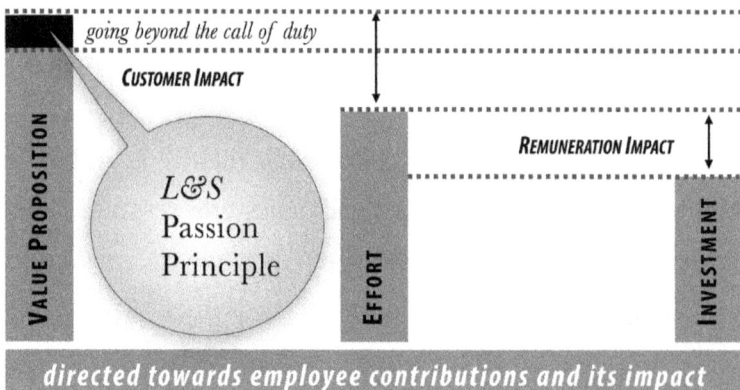

THE *L&S* SILENT PRINCIPLE

At the heart of the L&S Silent Principle the first Loyalty Axiom of Silence will always be central to employees. It is never about being in the spotlight.

The second Loyalty Axiom of Latitude is about the level of endurance and accommodation that employees are willing to go through. This is linked to the third Loyalty Axiom of Shared Values and Vision. All three axioms are inter related and could well have an interplay within the employee facing L&S Principles in precipitating a culture of service excellence.

Unseen and beyond the line of sight the correlation between employee facing L&S Principles and customer facing L&S Principles is an opportunity for new insights.

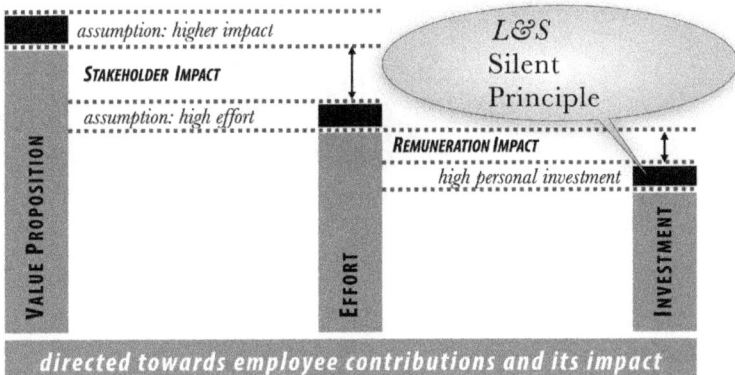

The unspoken contributions of these dedicated employees are inspired by a sense of shared values and vision that propels them to put the organization before their own priorities to create value for all stakeholders.

There's an interplay between the customer and employee facing *L&S Principles* — there should be some hidden insights that refined algorithms and approaches could possibly bring to fruition.

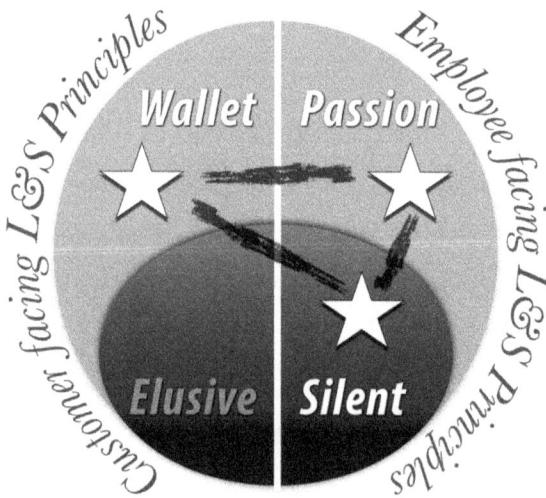

IN SUMMARY — GO FIGURE!

★ The central principle in any relationship is the reciprocal spirit of giving one's best for the other. This is universal to any relationship between spouses, siblings, families, clans or brands.

★ This chapter proposes using quotient of sacrifice as the kernel of loyalty in a robust cause and effect between value proposition, price paid and benefit derived rather than relying on heuristics or assumptions about surrogate measures of repeat purchase.

★ It is not just about what a customer gains from a transaction that determines their relationship with a product or service but is rather an equation of what or how much the customer is willing to accommodate, forgo, accept, and tolerate, for them.

★ Proposed here is a framework for a unified definition of loyalty with four principles that holistically encompass customer and employee loyalty.

5

He who does not understand your silence
will probably not understand your words.

— *Elbert Hubbard*

5. The *L&S* Elusive Principle

There are many who are not bargain hunters. They are loyal and willing to forgo and forgive. This does not mean they forget. Instead, they choose to compromise, lower their expectation on what is offered and then be satisfied in consuming or experiencing something that is lower than the original offer. This can only be explained due to the power of the brand in which the patrons have bestowed their trust. A confluence of shared values and shared vision that makes these customers willingly sacrifice and make concessions when faced with a situation that tests their loyalty.

In the real world, a customer is presented with a plethora of choices. At times hidden in these choices are compromises— instances when the customer is ready to make a sacrifice or overlook lapses, by choice, for a product or service, in the face of better options in their own mind. The more sacrifice the customer willingly makes, the greater their loyalty.

Over the years I have come across many anecdotes that I wish to share to illustrate the elusive nature of loyalty.

THE GRAND DAME OF NEW YORK

The Grand Dame of New York is one such example that made me reflect on this. On one of my visits to Manhattan my former colleague who was the General Manager of a fine luxury hotel in New York, shared one of his personal experiences as a hotelier.

A senior citizen used to visit our hotel for a silent stay many times a year. This lady was always fussing about something or the other. Nothing my team did could satisfy her. Yet, she always stayed at this hotel.

During one such visit, just after checking in, she started complaining about something trivial. So I sat her down and, over a cup of coffee, told her, "As much as we like you, my team is rather sad to see that even our best efforts don't seem enough to make you happy. So at no additional cost, I have booked a grand suite for you in the hotel across the street because I want you to be happy and satisfied."

Far from being pleased, the lady was a bit taken aback. When she recovered, she told me emphatically that she would most certainly not go to the hotel suite that I had booked for her; she would stay put in our hotel.

Subsequently, her complaints completely stopped even as she continued to stay at the hotel for that visit and on several visits thereafter. The hotel was her home away from home with many treasured memories and she did not want to part with it. When offered an alternative, this loyalist was willing to overlook the little things that were irritating her. She was willing to make all required compromises, to forgo and forgive.

The Reclusive CEO

There's another true story in the same vein from the hospitality industry. This is about a reclusive CEO who would not forget but was ready to forgive and forgo. This gentleman used to frequently stay at his preferred hotel. Prior to one such visit, he abruptly altered his plans due to a booking glitch and decided to never come back again to his favored hotel. The hotel staff was starkly aware of his non-demanding demeanor. Surprisingly it was the training manager who, perhaps going beyond the call of duty, reached out to this annoyed soul. He recalled that this guest was peculiar in that he was the opposite of the demanding customer. He preferred to keep to himself and never wanted any attention. He would refrain from accepting all the bells and whistles showered upon him and was never known to complain. *"So what on earth did the hotel staff do to him that landed us in this situation?"* the training manager wondered.

To find the answer, he tracked down the disgruntled CEO and visited the guest in his office to understand what had offended him. The guest offered an unexpected concern: *"I hope you don't run your hotel to the ground and go out of business."* *"Strange for a disgruntled guest to say that; after all, why should he care if the hotel business survives,"* the training manager thought to himself.

It turned out that the guest had extreme affection for this hotel. *"You have no idea,"* the guest said, *"of why this hotel has treasured memories for me. One of the most important meetings of my life that I ever attended was in the business center room in this hotel. It was my father who held this business meeting and it was the last time I ever saw my father. He died the next day. This meeting changed my life, and whenever I come to this hotel, I feel closer to him. I can pay top dollar and go to any other hotel as well. I pay what you demand — I never negotiate on rates."*

The training manager was stunned. He did not expect this response. It was unfathomable. While he was able to get the guest back and address his concerns, the takeaway for me was that the *axiom of silence* exists. The *elusive way* was at play. How many defining moments will it take to illustrate that customer loyalty exists in the most unexpected quadrants? This guest was willing to pay a higher share of wallet and yet was elusive about not demanding higher service levels.

Unless such experiences like that of the Grand Dame of New York and the Reclusive CEO are made part of the brand promise and guest experience by design, the presence and potency of elusive behavior will not be recognized. In both cases the customer was ready to forgive and forgo due to their deeply entrenched loyalty. Deep down there is trust and that's what truly matters.

A LIFELONG COMMITMENT

A family with a lifelong commitment to their favorite automaker had owned about 30 cars of the same brand over the past three decades. It was a brand they trusted and they would never settle for another ride. Everyone in the family drove cars from the same brand and they would not have it any other way. Even when one of the cars had problems with an ill-fitting floor mat that caused havoc with safety issues as it affected the accelerator, they didn't give up on the car.[5a] Instead they had it fixed and trusted their cherished brand to continue making reliable vehicles.

Another car owner who patronized the same auto brand for over 32 years stood by the brand even when his car was recalled over safety issues.[5b] He continued to believe that despite the recalls, his chosen brand still made the safest vehicles on the road. These loyal customers have so much faith in their preferred automaker that they are willing to forgive the brand for mishaps and implicitly trust it to fix all safety concerns.

Deep down such is the confidence in the brand. After all trust can be instilled with transparency and a confluence of shared values.

There's a plethora of studies about the impact of vehicle recalls on the automotive market that continues to aid decision making for executives in the industry. But are these professionals aware of such extraordinary, defining moments that pervades loyal customers who are ready to forgive and forgo?

There is no loyalty program that captures such sentiments. The surrogate measure for loyalty could very well be repeat purchase but the emotional response to the brand and the affection that is showered by loyalty that is characterized by a sense of elusiveness, is unparalleled. For these devoted owners, their car is more than just good looks, an engineering marvel or a vehicle of choice to meet their transportation needs. They are objects of affection, much like a family member, because the brand which makes them, can be trusted.

A SPEEDING TICKET DEFINES LOYALTY

There's an interesting anecdote[5c] I came across in an auto magazine about a resolute gentleman who never drove anything but a particular car that was an icon of automotive luxury and emblematic of much that defined America then — a rising middle class living in the suburbs for whom owning the car was a symbol of aspiration, achievement and success, of having arrived in life. The car lagged behind its competitors in performance, yet he remained loyal to the brand.

Once, while contesting a speeding ticket for his 1985 model, he defended himself by arguing that his car could not physically attain the speed he was clocked at unless he had a running start from the top of a mountain three states over. The judge accepted his defense and threw out the ticket, thereby validating the defendant's plea: *"My car is real slow."* In later years, the gentleman went on to own a newer model of the same brand which had severe torque steer deficiencies. Yet, he never lamented not buying any other car, because as far as he was concerned, they did not exist.

How else can we explain this forgo and forgive equation but to associate this loyalty factor to an elusive one? Are cult brands made of deep associations at the kernel of which is the ability to *sacrifice – and compromise?*

An Icon of Desire

One bike enthusiast[5d] coveted an iconic motorcycle brand as a kid and through his growing up years and early adulthood. In fact, he was almost 40 before he could save enough to buy the bike of his dreams from his boss. Even then there was one final hurdle to cross — he had to work for his boss for free for 18 months before he could call the bike his own.

This particular brand of motorcycle is not the best performing machine around. It is not the fastest or the neatest and it is definitely not environmental friendly. Plus it is super expensive to buy and maintain. And yet the brand evokes a cult following. Its logo is tattooed on more men than any other logo. To its owner, it is a work of art, and its price and functionalities are secondary.

FOR MOTIVATION & CAMARADERIE

My friend, a reluctant exerciser, lives in a luxury high-rise with its own state-of-the-art gym complete with top-of-the-range equipment for a variety of workouts. The thought of working out solo does not inspire her and so she joined a group of fitness enthusiasts who meet at a nearby community center where instructors hold structured, high-intensity, bootcamp style training sessions five days a week. A range of free weights, sand bags, jumping ropes, resistance tubes and medicine balls make up the equipment list at the community centre. No cardio theatre, TV display, locker or shower facilities, sauna or juice bar. Not even a filtered water station.

Membership for these 45 minute sessions is about $200 a month, steep compared to the many fancy gym franchises in her neighborhood which offer a ton of facilities at a much lower price. Yet, she doesn't mind paying the price premium. For her, the shared motivation, inspiration, accountability and emotional camaraderie make her bare bones group workouts more valuable than a bells and whistles gym membership. She's willing to pay a higher share of wallet and yet is elusive about not demanding better facilities which may give her more bang for the buck.

HEY, I AM LOYAL TO MY CLAN

Undoubtedly the comfort of basking in shared values has its virtues as well as drawbacks. A striking comment from the retired CEO of an engineering and technology business of a multinational conglomerate where he worked for many decades, says it all. This gentleman had invested a substantial part of his retirement savings in the financial services arm of the conglomerate that pursued wealth management. My conversation about the axioms of loyalty and its application to business evoked his positive acknowledgment of my proposed concept.

"Wow! Very thought provoking! And very useful for business leaders." — he said. He then continued, *"Let me give you my personal story to explain (my) sacrifice."* He elaborated how the portfolio manager assigned by the wealth management company was not up to speed. *"I am quite disappointed with their advice. There are many other reputed financial advisors and*

wealth managers. Why don't I change? It is clearly a 'sacrifice' for me, but hey, I am loyal to my clan..."

I wonder what else can explain this but the *Loyalty Axiom of Silence* and the *Loyalty Axiom of Shared Values and Vision*. These are elusive souls willingly accommodating as stated in the *Loyalty Axiom of Latitude*. Willing to let go. Willing to compromise silently.

PERSISTING PRACTICES HIDING IN PLAIN SIGHT

There is always an elasticity and inelasticity that dictates the level of attachment. Can the concept of price inelasticity be applied to share price? The only way the stock market describes itself is in terms of bulls and bears. Surely there is more to it than the animal instinct. The inelasticity due to the *Loyalty Axiom of Shared Values and Vision* for certain brands is a bullish behavior even in a falling bear market. These are elusive ones weathering the storm with longterm view affirming their loyalty despite losing short term value.

Deep clarity emerged once the definition of loyalty was enunciated in my mind with the four axioms. A glimmer of persisting practices knocking at the door to find a way to amplify missing priorities in defining loyalty surrounds a wealth of enlightenment in numerous concepts that readily apply to explain the *L&S Elusive Principle*. While the inelasticity of price as a concept can be readily applied to the *L&S Wallet Principle*, the persisting practices around the *L&S Elusive Principle* are becoming discernible as well.

Michel Hogan, an independent brand counsel, makes a cogent point in her article *"We're all human: Why customers need to be more forgiving"*. She concludes with a plea to customers:

> *So next time you're about to jump online and write a bad review or tweet about a perceived failure you feel is worth your wrath, please stop. Before you hit send, take a minute to wonder — just maybe whatever happened wasn't about you at all. Maybe somewhere, someone just like you made a mistake.*[5e]

Now that may corroborate with the *Axiom of Futility* as a customer can be expected to make compromises and accommodations only when there is a strong alignment of values with the brand, which drives loyalty and encourages the customer to overlook lapses and stick to the brand no matter what. But Ms. Hogan who rightly believes that an organization's brand is a result of various elements coming together, and has continually applied her mind to exploring these elements that contribute to the achievement, and how they relate to each other, should be admired and appreciated for her work.

In recent years there has been a growing interest in studying customer forgiveness following mistakes or lapses by a company, and its relation to loyalty. The Temkin Group analyzes the Net Promoter Score (NPS) — the popular customer loyalty metric — of companies across industries, based on responses from thousands of US customers on three areas of loyalty: likelihood to repurchase, likelihood to forgive, and the actual number of times they recommend a company. It also publishes the Temkin Forgiveness Ratings (TFR) which measures the willingness of a customer to forgive a company for its mistakes. The most recent TFR uses feedback from 10,000 U.S. consumers to rate how likely consumers are to forgive 318 organizations across 20 industries after they make a mistake. Companies in the Banking and Rental Cars & Transport industry scored highest with a TFR of 73%.[5f]

A paper titled "Customer Forgiveness following Service Failures" published in the *Current Opinion in Psychology* journal examines the unique aspects of customer forgiveness:

Recent research has focused on the conditions under which customers will forgive firms for their misdeeds. Within this context, it is important to recognize that some service failures represent minor issues that occur within routine customer-firm exchange relationships, while others represent severe issues that occur within well-established customer-firm communal relationships. We propose that the construct of 'customer forgiveness' becomes more relevant when there is a (1) relational norm violation within a strong customer-firm relationship; (2) severe service failure; (3) failed recovery (double deviation); and (4) a belief that the firm was trying to take advantage of the customer (negative inferred firm motives). Building on these ideas, we outline an integrative model of customer forgiveness in the wake of service failures.[5g]

In conclusion, there exists a plethora of knowledge around concepts and measurements that can fall within the ambit of the *L&S Elusive Principle*. It is only a question of connecting the dots and collaborating on ideas to craft a measurement of customer forgiveness that takes into account the four axioms of loyalty. It shouldn't be a one off study but a mainstream metric of customer loyalty covering the axioms of loyalty and the permissible scope of all four *L&S Principles*.

IN SUMMARY — THE *L&S* ELUSIVE PRINCIPLE

★ This chapter portrays stories that demonstrate that customers are willing to forgo and accommodate — due to a confluence of shared values and shared vision.

★ Such a strong alignment with shared values leads to a certain degree of sacrifice. Measuring such parameters could lead to a contextual matrix of loyalty. Intuitively forgiveness quotient exists in thought and in measurement practices in studying customer forgiveness.

★ Stories covered:

Title	Source
• *The Grand Dame of New York*	*Author's first hand account*
• *The Reclusive CEO*	*Author's first hand account*
• *A Lifelong Commitment*	*5a – CNN, Feb 4, 2010* *5b – ABC News, Feb 9, 2010*
• *A Speeding Ticket Defines Loyalty*	*5c – Car and Driver, Mar 17, 2016*
• *An Icon of Desire*	*5d – Quora, May 11, 2018*
• *For Motivation and Camaraderie*	*Author's first hand account*
• *Hey, I Am Loyal to my Clan*	*Author's first hand account*

6

You do not have to be rich to be generous.

—— *Anonymous*

6. THE *L&S* WALLET PRINCIPLE

elasticity
&
inelasticity

Generously sacrificing one's share of wallet is a well-known occurrence in purchasing. The reflex that often explains this generous payout of a premium is presumably due to the brand and its reputation. Or is this an instance of a marketer's heuristic thinking? Should we assume that everyone who pays a premium acts pragmatically and logically?

While sacrificing the share of wallet there are some who pay a higher premium even as they expect no more than what the brand has originally promised.

A collage of stories from my personal experiences and those unearthed through research explicitly amplify the appetite to sacrifice the share of wallet. Some know this as inelasticity of price.

THE DOCTOR FROM LONDON

A doctor from London told me about his favorite hotel and how he always looked forward to spending his family vacations there. His plea to the staff at the hotel was simple. *"Don't mess with my experience when I am on holiday. As a doctor I work hard. My vacation is the only time I get to relax, and it's your job to make me feel like royalty."* He was willing to pay a premium and give the hotel a higher share of his wallet for consistently giving him the kind of personalized experience he needed.

Discerning customers often know what it takes to get what they want. They are not bargain hunters. They pay generously and this is the share of wallet sacrifice they endure in order to display their loyalty. And yet there exists a blindspot in identifying the sacrifice dimension in the loyalty displayed. It is the share of wallet willingly sacrificed. Naysayers often explain in hindsight that the customer got what they paid for. That to me is turning a blind eye to this act of generosity. The conclusion is unavoidable: the premium paid by customers for a value that was not contracted can only be considered as arising from the *Loyalty Axiom of Silence* and *Loyalty Axiom of Shared Values and Vision*.

DISCERNING CUSTOMERS ARE WILLING

Discerning customers know what to ask, what is permissible, and are ready to sacrifice their share of wallet for what they want.

A couple cruising on a chartered mega yacht[6a] in the Aegean, one morning, unexpectedly insisted that an additional stewardess be brought on board to increase the service level. They also requested five cases of Louis Roederer Cristal champagne. Despite the challenges the requests posed, both were fulfilled within a few hours. A stewardess was flown in from Athens to the island where the yacht was docked that day. Five cases of champagne secured from Athens and Salonika — a city 188 miles north of Athens — were also delivered to the yacht on the same day.

A COLLAGE: REAFFIRMING SHARE OF WALLET

The world is an interesting place and service levels is all about meeting the expectations of customers as they sacrifice the share of their wallet and trust the service team to deliver. Numerous anecdotes amplify the validity of the *Share of Wallet* principle. A client of a private jet operator[6b] paid for their favorite Michelin star chef to cook them a meal in New York which was delivered by air to them in Chicago. Another exacting client[6c] wanted a 33-pound turkey to be bought in Dubai and delivered frozen to Saudi Arabia for a Thanksgiving dinner party in Jeddah the next night.

Even pets have had their food flown in! A lady in Florida[6d] who treated her beloved pooch to a particular brand of luxury dog-food had it flown from France on a private jet. She insisted that local varieties were not suitable for her dog's refined palette, and that the dog's behavior was different without this particular brand of dog food only available in France. For these customers, money is no object. They don't like to compromise on their experience and are willing to pay a price premium for the product or service they desire.

Songwriters Benny Andersson and Björn Ulvaeus said it all: *"Money, money, money — Must be funny — In the rich man's world — Money, money, money — Always sunny — In the rich man's world…"* The perceived value of money no matter what it is for the rich and famous ready to sacrifice their share of wallet, is nevertheless an important conversation to have so that essential factors of sacrifice can be discussed, understood and recognized.

HE LOVED HER FOR LIFE

Here's a true story that distressed me. It's about a guy who was out of work for months[6e] when he bought his coveted motorcycle. He was a tree trimmer. His wife had been a bartender and had just switched to cleaning houses for lucrative prospects. They lived in an old 1950s track house of about 1000 sq. ft. with dividers for interior walls and a poorly done homeowner add on room above the basement garage. This guy had taken out a line of credit on his house to buy his cherished bike. He was in his forties and wanted to have it while still young enough to enjoy it. They soon divorced and had to sell the house. But despite his misfortune his bike remained; even in adversity, he couldn't let go of his most prized possession.

How do cult brands recognize and reward such loyalty?
After all reciprocity is central to a longterm relationship.

IS THAT CUSTOMER INTIMACY?

A lady enamored with an exclusive, ultra-expensive, luxury handbag[6f] built a long-term relationship with the brand just to be offered the opportunity to buy one of the manufacturer's "it" bags. The first time she walked into the store she simply bought a scarf and a bracelet, and at the checkout, enquired about the bag she desired. She was told that they didn't have any available and was put on the waiting list along with her preference for size, color and finish. While she waited, every once in a while, she would stop by the store and buy something small, like a perfume or an agenda refill, just so she could check in and see if they had any in stock. About 18 months and thousands of dollars later she was finally informed that a bag was available. It wasn't the specifications she wanted but she decided to buy it anyway and loved her purchase. She wanted the bag so much that to acquire it, she bought products that she probably didn't even need. For the love of the bag, she generously gave her share of wallet to the brand.

An interesting paradox of the digital age of today is that while credit ratings can alert a seller about the inadequate credit score of a customer and decline them a new store credit card, yet, that information cannot be used to recognize sacrifice quotient.

Are cult brands designed to extract a high share of wallet thereby inducing such sacrifice?

Is stretching the price inelasticity a surrogate measure of sacrificing the share of wallet?

SUMMARY — THE *L&S* WALLET PRINCIPLE

★ Customers have always had an appetite for sacrificing their share of wallet. It is measurable and a body of knowledge around price inelasticity exists.

★ Cult brands have perfected the art of extracting the share of wallet that could induce sacrifice beyond the marketers' line of sight.

★ Stories covered:

Title	*Source*
• *The Doctor From London*	*Author's first hand account*
• *Discerning Customers are Willing*	*6a – James D. Roumeliotis, Montreal, Canada*
• *A Collage: Reaffirming Share of Wallet*	*6b – The Telegraph, Sep 1, 2016* *6c – Mel Magazine* *6d – Observer, Aug 9, 2016*
• *He Loved Her for Life*	*6e – Prairie Eco-Thrifter, Apr 6, 2012*
• *Is That Customer Intimacy?*	*6f – Vox, Jun 26, 2015*

7

*Only an extraordinary person
can turn opportunity into reality.*

— *Aleksandr Solzhenitsyn*

7. THE *L&S* PASSION PRINCIPLE

how legends
are
created

In the realm of employee tribulations towards delighting customers somewhere resides the potential to act with courage and pride by going beyond the call of duty. Despite investment of necessary costs in the business the defining moments and value for customers is created by the effort put in by employees. The magic of value creation for stakeholders or specifically for customers has captivating nuances illustrated through anecdotes that reaffirm passion and perseverance.

I CAN HEAR YOU LOUD AND CLEAR

Without passion and a steadfast belief in the organization's vision and sharing the organizational values, great service is just an aspiration. Great customer service requires a business to make sure all its customers feel welcome. A regular customer, who was hearing impaired,[7a] used to give his order at his local coffee shop by typing it on his phone and showing it to the barista. One day, the barista surprised him by using sign language to ask for his order. And then she puzzled and delighted the customer by handing a note that read *"I've been learning the American Sign Language just so you can have the same experience as everyone else."*

She wasn't required to do this; yet she equipped herself with what she felt was necessary to make her customer's experience better. Investing one's personal time and effort to learn the sign language translates into a higher level of effort by the employee which greatly impacted the value proposition for the stakeholder touched and delighted by this effort.

The body of knowledge assimilated around brand affinity as a marketer's tool know that it is a valuable asset. This is an inside out phenomena and the affinity starts with employees and permeates into customer brand affinity. Mature leaders know that when internal affinity dissipates it can erode customer brand affinity.

DARN! I DROPPED MY PASSPORT IN A MAILBOX

Loyalty to one's profession is a reality and can coexist with loyalty to the cause as well. As evident from this heartwarming narrative of a passenger who had accidentally dropped her passport[7b] into an airport mailbox along with some mail and was certain she'd be stuck for days before she could fly. One can't imagine the barrage of emotions that she would have experienced. *Imagine that!* Dropping your passport in a mailbox while traveling overseas? Where do you even begin to decide what to do next?

Luckily, an airline employee came to her rescue, handling her problem as though it were his own. He went out of his way to get her a special travel approval from the authorities, convinced the airline staff to accept her baggage and issue a boarding pass, and finally, escorted her through passport control and security, explaining her plight to the officers and encouraging them to let her board her flight. Then, to make sure that the passport would be returned to the airline after it was retrieved, he taped a note on the mailbox for the postal worker. A few days later, the lady got her passport back by FedEx.

In her words, this experience was *"a true customer-service miracle made entirely possible by one dedicated employee."* The employee could have easily asked her to come back after she recovered her passport; it wouldn't have been remiss of him to do that. Instead he went out of his way and made every effort to ensure that the passenger was able to board her flight. In this act of going beyond the call of duty he made his company's brand proposition come alive for the passenger in a real, tangible way.

Some may wonder if this is an incident from another time and another place in history as it is beyond comprehension given the perils of security issues of the present day and age. This incident was reported in June, 2013 and involved crossing the Atlantic Ocean as the passport was dropped in Paris at the Charles de Gaulle airport mailbox. Up close was the first problem to address, and that was to calm the increasing panic that the lady was experiencing. It certainly wasn't a cakewalk to address all that would be required to get the U.S. Homeland Security Customs and Border Control representative involved and resolutions reached to get the problem solved. The power of passion for doing what it takes to solve problems is at the heart of this story and is a true illustration of passion and perseverance.

Living by the Company's Credo

For one sales associate at a large departmental store,[7c] providing outstanding service was not just a company credo. It was in total alignment with her own belief system — a perfect match of values of the employee and the organization. When a frazzled and overwhelmed husband wanted help in finding the perfect gift for his wife who had recently become a new mother, this 16-year-old associate helped him pick up a lovely outfit, only to find that they didn't have his wife's size in stock.

The sales associate waited till her shift ended at 5 pm, and then drove for an hour to another location of the store, picked up the desired size and then personally delivered the wrapped outfit to the customer's home the same evening. She could have simply directed the person to the next store but instead she chose to take her company's credo of *"providing outstanding service to a customer"* a step further, and by going out of her way to meet her customers' need, she created a memorable experience for them. Her loyalty to the organization, its cause and to her profession are a result of her passion and perseverance

LEARNING TO SPEED DIAL

This was also evident in the case of the call centre representative of a telecom company[7d] who received a query from an elderly customer asking for help programming her phone so she could use the speed dial feature. The representative immediately suggested looking up the phone's operation manual which was available online. The lady, however, neither owned a computer, nor had access to one.

Not one to give up, he made a copy of the manual and visited the customer's house to show her how to program her phone. He also spoke with her about her phone plan and suggested an alternative that better matched her needs. By the time he left, she had a new, less expensive phone plan, a phone manual and was ready to speed-dial. Needless to say she was deeply thankful to the call centre representative for taking the initiative and doing more than his duties entailed, to help out a customer.

SHE TRACKED HIM DOWN — HE WAS IMPRESSED

Sometimes great customer service plays out through impromptu gestures. When a person lost his glasses on a train,[7e] he immediately ordered a new pair, sure that he wouldn't get his old ones back. A few weeks later, he was surprised to receive a package that contained two pairs of glasses and a handwritten note from an employee of the brand whose glasses he wore.

It turns out she was on the same train as he and after he got off, noticed that he had left his glasses behind. So she tracked him down and sent him a fresh pair of glasses along with his old ones. The gentleman was so impressed that he posted about the experience on Facebook, *"They have a customer for life!"* For the employee, her duty towards the customer didn't stop even after she had left her workplace.

This is the essence of passion and perseverance at work — displaying loyalty that emanates from believing in the cause the company was founded upon: to offer designer eyewear at a revolutionary price, while leading the way for socially conscious business. The values upon which the company motto was built stems from an experience narrated on the company website: *"We were students when one of us lost his glasses on a backpacking trip. The cost of replacing them was so high that he spent the first semester of grad school without them, squinting and complaining. (We don't recommend this.) The rest of us had similar experiences, and we were amazed at how hard it was to find a pair of great frames that didn't leave our wallets bare. Where were the options?"* Clearly, these values resonated with the employee and inspired her best efforts.

ABOUT LIFE SUPPORT

Human beings are innately risk averse, and, when assessing their options, will err towards caution. This is particularly so in their workplace. But when there's a strong connection between their organizational and personal values it helps them see their work as meaningful and encourages them to go beyond expectations and make a difference. Like in the case of this particular airline pilot who put his job on the line[7f] to help a distraught passenger.

This passenger was on his way from a business trip to his daughter's home to see his comatose three-year-old grandson who was being taken off life support that evening so his organs could be used to save other lives. The passenger's wife called the airline to arrange the last-minute flight and explained the emergency.

Unfortunately, the man was first held up in traffic and then delayed due to long lines at the airport. The passenger reached the boarding gate 12 minutes after the plane was scheduled to depart and was shocked to find the pilot waiting for him.

The pilot knew the passenger's story and refused to take off without having the distressed man on board. He was sensitive to the man's emergency and at the cost of losing his job, had willingly decided to delay the flight. When the passenger was profuse in his gratitude to the pilot, he replied, *"They can't go anywhere without me, and I wasn't going anywhere without you. Now relax. We'll get you there. And again, I'm so sorry."* Thanks to the pilot, the man reached his grandson in time to say his final goodbye.

We all know how paranoid airlines are about being punctual. Airlines compete with each other on securing the best on-time departure record and employees are evaluated based on their ability to keep to the schedule. Most airlines would punish an employee for holding up a flight. But fortunately for this pilot, his employers supported his decision and held his action as exemplary. His decision may have been personal and spur-of-the-moment but it was driven by the company's credo to *"connect people to what's important in their lives"* — a perfect alignment of values driving loyalty.

THE PHARMACY GOT INVOLVED

Consider the case of this teenage passenger whose cabin luggage was checked in[7g] by the flight crew due to lack of overhead space but who failed to collect it before boarding his connecting flight. When he landed at his destination, obviously he could not find his bag in the baggage carousel. But the airlines also couldn't track it down as he didn't have a claim number since it wasn't a checked bag.

He had given up all hopes of recovering his bag. So imagine his surprise when he got a call from his local pharmacy concerning his lost bag. Apparently the lost and found baggage member at the connecting airport where his bag was left, found his prescription in his bag, got his name and number and called him. Since he didn't answer the call, she called his pharmacy and requested them to inform him that they had found his bag and would ship it to him once he gave the airline a call. Talk about dedication! The airlines employee didn't give up when she couldn't reach the passenger directly. Instead she looked for other ways to reach him and at the end made sure he got his bag back.

WHERE THERE IS NO STRUGGLE, THERE IS NO STRENGTH

In another instance of missed airlines baggage, a passenger was separated from her luggage[7h] when she was able to catch an earlier, direct flight home. Her bags, which had been on her original flight, was going to be couriered to her home later that evening. However, due to maintenance problems, that flight was canceled and her luggage was stuck.

The lady was anxious as her suitcase not only contained her medication but also her comfort items, including a rosary she had with her for every chemotherapy treatment she went to, and a T-shirt that read *"Where there is no struggle, there is no strength"*. The contents of the bag were especially important because she had a chemotherapy appointment the very next morning. She wanted to wear the T-shirt to her treatment and without the rosary, she would have felt *"distraught and uncomfortable and scared."*

She eventually got in touch with an airline employee at the airport and explained to her why she needed her luggage at the earliest. The employee assured her that she would track down the luggage and if it came in that night, would make sure a courier delivered it to the lady's home. However, the luggage arrived after the last courier had left for the night.

That's when the airline employee decided to do something totally unexpected. She personally drove to the lady's home at three in the morning and left the luggage at her doorstep with a note apologizing for the delay and wishing the lady luck for her treatment. She was under no obligation to do that nor was it part of her job description, yet the employee, recognizing the urgency of the situation, chose to go beyond the expected and help a distraught customer.

True loyalty is marked by a quiet dedication to the cause; it's never about being in the spotlight or aspiring to be rewarded or crowned *'employee of the month'*. While acts of self-sacrifice in the line of duty are not desirable, one cannot help but be humbled by such acts that are beyond words.

Suppressing Personal Grief

Take the case of this stoic employee who worked in a boutique hotel's kitchen. Since it was peak tourist season, the hotel had high occupancy and was booked right up till early January. On December 20, he received devastating news from his family, informing him that his seven month old daughter had passed away. Knowing that his presence was critical to keep the kitchen running smoothly during the busy season, he kept the unfortunate news to himself and quietly went about performing his duties. It was only on January 3rd that he informed his manager about his situation who then immediately made arrangements for him to leave and be with his family. No one had asked him to do this, but he was so much a part of the service culture that without a moment's hesitation, he was willing to put aside his personal grief to fulfill his duties at work.

DIAMONDS ARE FOREVER

Indeed, when there is genuine dedication and alignment of values, going beyond what is expected, becomes *'part of the job'*. When a lady reached home from one of her many visits to her favorite fashion store, she realized that the diamond from her wedding ring was missing.[7i] She rushed back to the store and started looking for the diamond in all the places she picked her clothes from.

An employee of the store, out on his routine rounds, saw her frantically searching for something, and clearly in distress. He offered to help her, but even after spending hours searching the store, they couldn't find her diamond and the lady returned home extremely distraught. The employee however, refused to give up and got in touch with two workers from the building services team. Together they again rummaged through all the vacuum cleaner bags, searching through the dust and debris till they finally found the diamond.

The lady was overwhelmed with gratitude on getting her diamond back, *"I had insurance…it could have been replaced. But to have my diamond back! It meant the world to me!"* The employee felt humbled to realize how a 'small' effort from his side could have such a huge impact for his customer.

The lady acknowledged that this act of kindness and customer centric behavior clearly reflected the values of the company he worked for — an alignment of values impelling loyalty, thereby underlining the deep connect with passion and perseverance.

PIZZA ORDER WITH TOPPINGS OF DEVOTION

Almost every night for over 10 years, a customer used to order a late dinner from his local pizza store.[7j] He had no signature order — sometimes he would call for a salad, sometimes a pie, sometimes chicken wings — the only thing the staff knew for sure was that his name would show up on their online ordering site sometime between 11 p.m. and midnight several times a week. So when his orders suddenly stopped, the pizza store's manager checked and saw that it had been 11 days since he had last ordered, which was unlike him. She had known him since she was a delivery driver and regularly made the short trip to his home about six minutes away. She knew he worked from home and rarely left his house. She also knew that he had suffered some health issues in the past. She could not help thinking that something was wrong. So she sent one of her delivery drivers to check in on the customer at his home. When no one answered the door, the delivery guy called the customer on his phone which went straight to voicemail. Seriously worried now, he informed his manager, who called 911 for help. When the officers arrived and broke the door open, they found the customer on the floor and in need of immediate medical attention. One day later, and they might have been too late.

The customer recuperated in the hospital and while he was profuse in his gratitude for the pizza store manager's huge role in saving his life, for her it was all just part of the job. As she put it: *"He is just an important customer that's part of our family here … He orders all the time so we know him. I think we were just doing our job checking in on someone we know who orders a lot. We felt like we needed to do something."* Indeed this pizza order had toppings of devotion.

The manager's role was to ensure that the store operations went smooth, deliveries were on time, customers were happy and any concerns were addressed. But in this case, she really went beyond what was expected of her. She truly cared about her customers and her attentiveness helped saved a life.

IN SUMMARY — THE *L&S* PASSION PRINCIPLE

★ In the realm of employee tribulations towards delighting customers somewhere resides the potential to act with courage and pride by going beyond the call of duty.

★ Knowledge assimilated around brand affinity is a valuable asset. This is an inside out phenomena and the affinity starts with employees and permeates into brand affinity. Cutting edge marketing practices recognize that when internal affinity dissipates it can erode customer brand affinity.

★ Stories covered:

Title	Source
• *I Can Hear You Loud and Clear*	*7a – Starbucks, Feb 26, 2016*
• *Darn! I Dropped my Passport in a Mailbox*	*7b – Fast Company, Jun 14, 2013*
• *Living by the Company's Credo*	*7c – Salesforce Blog, May 8, 2014*
• *Learning To Speed Dial*	*7d – Times Colonist, Jan 22, 2016*

- *She Tracked Him Down – He Was Impressed*   7e – Forbes, Aug 1, 2014

- *About Life Support*   7f – CNN, Jan 14, 2011

- *The Pharmacy Got Involved*   7g – Minnie Gupta, Boston, USA

- *Where There is No Struggle, There is No Strength*   7h – Today, Aug 9, 2017

- *Suppressing Personal Grief*   Author's first hand account

- *Diamonds Are Forever*   7i – Customer Guru

- *Pizza Order With Toppings of Devotion*   7j – HuffPost, Nov 5, 2016

8

Silence is a gift. Learn to value its essence.

— Anonymous

those
magnificent
men &
women

Speech is silver and silence is golden is indeed a healthy indicator of relationships. We have established that the first axiom of loyalty is silence. Knowing when to speak and when to let go and embrace silence is a mark of the wise. The second is the *Loyalty Axiom of Shared Values and Vision*. Besides, action speaks louder than words. This characteristic of loyalty epitomizes discreet self-sacrifice for a larger cause. An alignment of values and vision propels such acts to create a higher value for stakeholders.

What explains such a force that permeates the mortal soul and creates value for everyone that is touched? Divine intervention, some may say. It is a human trait encompassing self-sacrifice, and willingness to adjust or accommodate, and yet, it is intended to be silent and never about being in the spotlight. The ability to forgo and forgive is about golden silence. Stories in this chapter reaffirm two out of the four axioms of loyalty — silence and shared values and shared vision.

THE RELUCTANT HEIR: DETERMINED TO SUCCEED

At the age of 44, a lady whose joy and passion lay in opening and running pre-schools,[8a] suddenly found herself in charge of running the family business her parents had started. It wasn't part of her life plan, and she had no interest in it. As a young girl, she used to help out at the company — which specialized in the production of sportswear — during summer breaks and after graduating from college. But she had never harbored any intention of a career in the family business.

However, when her father passed away, she reluctantly took over the reins on her mother's prodding. Presumably she had no siblings. Her first formidable challenge was to win the trust of the senior staff who had worked for the company for decades. Before she could make any changes she needed to convince them that she knew the challenges and opportunities of the business and that she knew what she was talking about when she spoke about the changes that needed to be made for the business to grow and prosper.

Not surprisingly, for the first few years nobody would listen to her, and, expectedly, she felt like giving up the company and running away. Gradually, however, she worked through the hurdles, even as she rapidly learned about the industry from the long-time employees. Eventually, her perseverance paid off and under her stewardship, they opened new factories, doubled their employee force, and increased their revenues.

Though she was passionate about her first career and would have achieved success there, she had unwillingly taken up the job out of a sense of duty to her parents, sacrificing her career and her dreams though eventually she reconciled her duty with her passion, with much success. The mysteries of human behavior is incomprehensible and is intriguing at many levels with many unanswered questions. The bottom line is that — an act of self sacrifice embraces a determination to succeed, eventually garnering value for all stakeholders.

SUSTAINING A THOUSAND YEAR LEGACY

Succession planning is never an easy task. Corporations struggle to develop a robust succession planning process. The *golden rule — whoever has the gold makes the rules* — may sound facetious but is true. When succession planning goes wrong it can alter a perfectly sustainable trajectory of an organization. Electing a successor to a successful business can be challenging. The one at the helm of the organization often imprints the values *(of his or her)* personality. They often dictate their own priorities that could easily result in the demise of the organization. It takes cognizance of selfless sacrifice to put the organization before one's personal priority, sometimes temporarily and sometimes permanently for life.

It is interesting to observe how the *loyalty axiom of shared values and vision* and the *loyalty axiom of silence* played a role for over a thousand years, in how a traditional Japanese organization rooted in tradition, worked. Hōshi Ryokan, a notable Japanese hotel built above a hot springs is 1,300 years old. Ownership and management is given exclusively to one person; other children are not involved. Throughout its epic history, the ryokan *(the Japanese name for this kind of hotel)* has always been owned by the Hōshi family. Hōshi means Buddhist priest, and the hotel started as a monastery. The monk who lived there adopted a son named Zengoro, and since then each subsequent generation has named the son who will own the hotel after him. Usually the first-born son inherits but if he declines or is not capable, and no other son is available, the position is offered to a daughter's husband, who is adopted by the family, who then takes the Hōshi name, leaving his own family behind. If there are no children, a successor is adopted into the family and takes over the ryokan.

The current Zengoro belongs to the 46th generation of the Hoshi family. His only son, who had been working at the ryokan in preparation of succeeding his father, passed away in 2013. His son's death upended the career path of his daughter, who had to give up her job and take over many of the management responsibilities at the hotel.

The current Zengoro hopes his daughter will step up to the plate, but it's an honor that she doesn't seem too keen to accept. As a carefree young woman, she had been on the look-out for a partner, hoping to find love, and was eager to move out of her family's orbit once she got married. But with the change in circumstances, her dreams have gone awry. She is now introduced to only those men who can be adopted into the Hōshi family. *"... There have been times that I wished I hadn't been born as a member of Hōshi. Before I started working at Hōshi Ryokan I graduated from university and worked as a doctor's secretary. I was learning what I was interested in. (Today) I have many unimaginable responsibilities and it is a heavy burden on my mind. I think I'm a weak person but people close to me think I'm a mentally strong person. I cry often."* [8b]

If her parents manage to find her a suitable husband, he could become the inn's 47th owner. If not, she may break with tradition and run it herself. For now, she continues to work silently alongside her parents, helping them run the inn and provide good hospitality. Her aging father has just one priority: finding a successor. *"Some things are more important than individual desires. Sometimes we have to sacrifice (for the) family. To keep the hot spring and the hotel running our daughter is the right person to do it. We will be waiting for her."*

AGENCY-MAN MASTERS THE GRILL

When the road chosen for a person by their legacy diverges from the path they would have picked, what does one do? Sometimes, the family business comes calling when one has already established themselves elsewhere — but a sense of obligation makes it tough to refuse. While some feel frustrated and trapped enough to want out, there are those who accept the situation and give up their own interests, and, inspired by a common set of values, silently go about fulfilling their obligations to the best of their ability.

A successful ad agency guy was relieved when his brother took up the mantle of managing the family's barbecue joint founded by their grandfather in 1949. *"I saw this as the linchpin — the thing that that would allow me to stay away".*[8c]

As a young boy, he used to help his father by sweeping floors and hauling out trash at the restaurant. But he had always longed to get away. *"I couldn't wait to get out ... (of there). To leave, never come back, put this whole barbecue thing behind me."* So he went to college, earned a degree and was happy running an ad agency when, one day, his father reached out to him for help.

The business was near bankruptcy under his brother's shaky stewardship, and his father summoned him home to help extricate his brother, hold off the creditors, and rebuild the business. It was either that, or let the place go to ruin, said the father.

In ways that he could not have foreseen or imagined, the thought of losing the family business shook him.

I didn't realize how much of my own personal history and ideas about life were tied into that place. When it was threatened, that became truly valuable to me.

When I got there, my father asked me to make a promise. He said, 'When I'm gone, you promise that you will keep this going.' How are you going to say no? You just put everything on the line on their behalf. You're vested now. You can't say no.

He reassigned his agency clients to other people and became a full-time barbecue guy. *"I was finally ready to do it. I'd seen and done many of the things I wanted to do. I felt I could come back; that I'd let go of that animosity, those feelings that I'd lost a childhood to this monolith."* While his decision to join the business was spurred by his father's call for help, today he's fully invested in his choice and determined to continue the family tradition.

A LOVE HATE RELATIONSHIP

The lady managing New York city's acclaimed pizzeria is in a similar quandary. The place was started by her father and is so popular that long lines of people wait outside for a slice of the pie handcrafted by the founder himself. After successfully running the place for over five decades, the patriarch's advancing age has the family concerned about the future of the pizzeria. While she manages the place now, with help from her siblings, she was never keen on the job.

I definitely have a love-hate relationship with the place; it's bittersweet. [8d]

When they were young, all six siblings had to work at the pizzeria every day after school, which annoyed them.

As teenagers we felt resentment because we had to put in so many hours there. It was expected of us, and we weren't able to make our own choices. Those are years we can't get back.

Later, she worked elsewhere but came back to help her father. Despite her conflicted feelings, she's worried about what would happen to the family business when her father passed, and later, when she and her brothers retired.

You can't force people into liking the things that you like, or caring about the things that you care about, but I honestly believe the place needs to stay in the family. Many years from now, when my dad is not with us anymore, the worst thing we could become is just a regular pizzeria.

Loyalty to family demands obedience and sacrifice. In fact, sacrifice is common in family life but most times it is so discreet that we often fail to notice it. It can be *active* (doing something against your own inclination in order to please someone you love) or *passive* (not doing something that you'd like to do in order to please someone you love).

It may seem costly at times, but when there's a confluence of shared values and vision, sacrifice leaves one full rather than empty — this is at the heart of the loyalty and sacrifice inherent in the four *L&S Principles*.

IN SUMMARY — THE *L&S* SILENCE PRINCIPLE

★ Employees' silent sacrifice exists. This characteristic of loyalty epitomizes discreet self-sacrifice for a larger cause. An alignment of values and vision propels such acts to create a higher value for stakeholders.

★ The interconnectedness of loyalty factors displayed by customers and employees have a correlation and could well be a subject for further study to establish empirical cause and effect given the common unified definition of loyalty.

★ Stories covered:

Title	Source
• *The Reluctant Heir: Determined to Succeed*	*8a – BBC, Nov 10, 2015*
• *Sustaining a Thousand Year Legacy*	*8b – Vimeo, 2014*
• *Agency-Man Masters the Grill*	*8c – Madfeed, Apr 8, 2015*
• *A Love Hate Relationship*	*8d – Madfeed, Apr 8, 2015*

9

*Sometimes I'm confused
by what I think is really obvious.
But what I think is really obvious
obviously isn't obvious ...*

— *Michael Stipe*

9. THE LATENCY FACTOR

digging deep
for why it
happened?

Unfathomable for some as to why the definition of 'loyalty' is skewed for customers and gathers a different meaning in other walks of life. This has to do with strong patterns of adherence to usage. The stronger the usage the more distorted its meaning tends to become. This is rooted in reality as proposed by Dr. Edward de Bono that information organized in patterns becomes a deterrent to new ideas. The more firmly the pattern is established, the harder it becomes to break away from established notions.

THE PERSISTING DISTORTIONS

Word meanings evolve due to pattern of usage, at times radically altering the original meaning so that words that were pure and simple get tainted with a definitive meaning that was never intended. A recent example that demonstrates how word meanings evolve and connotations change, came to the fore when French President Emmanuel Macron, speaking at a ceremony to commemorate the 100th anniversary of Armistice Day, declared, *"Patriotism is exactly the opposite of nationalism ... Nationalism is a betrayal of patriotism."*

These two words that were synonymous and largely interchangeable from the end of the 18th century onward for a number of decades, were used when referring to a general love for one's country. That changed in the 20th century, when the word 'nationalism' became associated with ethnic-supremacy movements in many countries. Wonder if all those who died in World War I could ever envisage that *Patriotism* would one day become the exact *opposite of nationalism* and that *Nationalism* would be seen as a *betrayal of patriotism*. A second painful death for all the fallen unable to understand such polarization of words in the age we live. Sanity prevails in the human mind in building blocks of logic, and yet, we have such distortions.

LEARNING FROM THE GURUS

While the definitions of certain words have developed as an assertion of the milieu, some words are derived from ideas based on plausible assumptions for developing the subject and open the door for a contextual conversation. And then there are instances of words where the meaning is bootstrapped to a predefined concept thereby shutting the door for enhancing its boundaries.

To explain these anomalies the concept of *The Latency Principle* was born in my mind. Human thinking is, on the one hand, about perception, and on the other, having perceived a stimulus, hoping to do something about it by acting on the perception. This results in the process of doing things and this act of doing reinforces the idea that you have acted upon. This makes it a spiral. A pattern.

Influenced by Dr. Edward de Bono's views on how to think about '*thinking*', I realized that a high share of effort is devoted to the process side of thinking. However, the most significant part of thinking is in the perception area. Besides, a high rate of repetitive reinforcement cements a certain pattern thereby making it difficult to break away from the patterns of thinking.

As we saw earlier, the more firmly a pattern of thinking is established, the harder it becomes to dissolve old notions. This is perhaps the very reason as to why a simple word like loyalty acquired different connotations — one for war veterans and employees and the other for customers. While sacrifice as a test of loyalty is expected from the former, it is unfathomable that a customer is capable of sacrifice. It is only fitting to settle a common and uniform definition for loyalty factors with inherent tendencies to forgo and forgive something. In his book *P.O: Beyond Yes and No,* Dr. Edward de Bono rightfully points out:

> *... P.O is the magic word ... it will do all you want it to do if you believe in it. As with all magic, the more you believe the better it works. The more you invest in it the more you get out of it. But there is no dogma you have to accept before you can use P.O. It is a simple word, and all you have to believe in is its use.*

Nobel-prize winning psychologist, social scientist and economist Herbert A. Simon, whose body of interdisciplinary work spanned the fields of cognitive science, computer science, public administration, management, and political science, was best known for his pioneering research into the human decision-making and problem-solving processes, and the implications of these processes for social institutions. He suggested that while people strive to make rational choices, human judgment is subject to cognitive limitations. Purely rational decisions would involve weighing such factors as potential costs against possible benefits. But people are limited by the amount of time they have to make a choice as well as the amount of information they have at their disposal. Other factors such as overall intelligence and accuracy of perceptions also influence the decision-making process.

Herbert A. Simon's work has unveiled a universal definition of Heuristics:

> *Heuristics are simple, efficient rules, hard-coded by evolutionary processes or learned, which have been proposed to explain how people make decisions, come to judgments, and solve problems, typically when facing complex problems or incomplete information. These are mental shortcuts and rule-of-thumb strategies that shorten decision-making time and allow people to solve problems and make judgments quickly and efficiently.*

Decision making often is based on two factors. It considers sound assumptions from past experiences on the one hand and on the other hand, it grapples with the nuances of the present environment and the future potential tendencies that are anticipated in the environment.

PROPOSING THE LATENCY PRINCIPLES

Leaning on the rich experiences and body of knowledge created by Dr. Edward de Bono and Herbert A. Simon, I was inspired to enunciate *The Latency Principle*. I recognize that there will be building blocks that define the attributes that will be responsible for characterizing the tendencies of concepts towards which the decision is hurled.

There are multiple factors that conjure up the perception of an idea or a concept. These factors are the basic building blocks and I have put together a checklist of four factors that characterizes the concept. The *Latency Principle* with these building blocks finds a scale from one extreme to the other extreme and is expressed in two parts: the *Hindsight-Latency* and the *Foresight-Latency* principles. The range stretches from justifying a compelling argument on reasonable grounds with plausible assumptions to open doors for progress, or shutting an argument with myopic assumptions riddled by adherence to patterns and mental shortcuts. The components that define these two diagonally opposite concepts of *Hindsight* and *Foresight Latency* reside in the foundation of the four building blocks.

1. **THE COGNITIVE BIAS**

   Ideas that are evolved heuristically with a *cognitive bias* — as mental shortcuts devoid of a firm logical step of evaluation.

2. **PRISONER TO STIGMA OR PATTERNS OF USAGE**

   Ideas that are reinforced due to strong conformance and or due to adherence to strong past usage pattern. Herd mentality of sorts.

3. **FACT BASED EMPIRICAL TENDENCIES**

   Ideas that lean on empirical evidence of cause and effect. Enough body of knowledge backs correlation and therefore the idea appears to be convincing.

4. **INTERDISCIPLINARY LEARNING**

   Ideas that have the benefit of being enriched by the infusion of interdisciplinary contributions.

Hindsight-Latency lacks integrity of empirical evidence, is heuristic in nature and prisoner to mental patterns of conformance. In contrast, *Foresight-Latency* allows comprehension of new ideas based on empirical evidence and sound plausible assumptions that open doors for a contextual conversation as it has the benefit of interdisciplinary contributions.

THE PERSISTENCE OF HINDSIGHT-LATENCY

Within the orbit of the *Hindsight-Latency Principle* words such as *Patriotic* is preferred and *Nationalist* is not. The phrase *Colored People* is incorrect. Instead, *People of Color* is acceptable. There are many words that have fallen prey to changes in meaning, like *Gay*, *Handicapped*, etc. It is a pretty long list of words that ought not be used. A recent outbreak of moral policing occurred at the US Center for Disease Control and Prevention (CDC) when the Trump administration banned officials from using seven words. According to news widely reported in the media, CDC leaders told employees that in official documents being prepared for the budget, they were forbidden to use words such as *diversity*, *vulnerable*, *evidence-based* and *transgender*. There are words and phrases such as *pro-choice* and *pro-life*. Every single one of these words, phrases and concepts connect to one or more of the four building blocks described in the *Latency Principle*.

Many definitions, phrases, ideas and words that have fallen prey to the *Hindsight-Latency Principle* perpetually surround us. *Hindsight-Latency* is used by climate change deniers and climate change proponents equally to lash back and forth. So long as the intention is to circumvent and explain a

	Hindsight Latency	Foresight Latency
COGNITIVE BIAS	Yes	*No*
PRISONER TO STIGMA OR PATTERNS OF USAGE	Yes	*No*
FACT BASED EMPIRICAL TENDENCIES	*No*	Yes
INTERDISCIPLINARY LEARNING TENDENCIES	*No*	Yes

phenomena by cherry picking facts and leaning on convenient assumptions, *Hindsight-Latency* will persist.

THE ALLURE OF FORESIGHT-LATENCY

In contrast, concepts, phrases and words are embraced by *Foresight-Latency*. These are least regimented but are permitted to plausible assumptions and scientific empirical grounds, not to circumvent or restrict a predetermined meaning but to further the conversation on a subject. The concept of *'Technological Singularity'* that has galvanized conversations is one such example.

MAPPING THE LATENCY-FACTORS

In human progress ideas will be considered and evaluated based on plausible empirical evidence or compelling theories. The gamut of ideas and concepts can be mapped on a scale ranging from *Hindsight-Latency* to *Foresight-Latency*. Ideas that are developed without stigma or bias are examples of *Foresight-Latency*. They come to fruition based on tendencies to open doors for a conversation. The idea of a united Europe or the EU as we know today started as an idea that was deliberated upon to open minds and possibilities over a long period. The development of the United Nations after WWII has a mandate to serve a noble cause.

A recent example — the longest US government shutdown in 2018–19 — clearly demonstrates *Hindsight-Latency*. It was riddled by heuristic tendencies — stigma and patterns bred the belief that building a wall on the southern US border would solve drug trafficking and illegal immigration as an optics for the voter base.

Brexit was yet another case of *Hindsight-Latency* that manipulated the messaging to evoke a desirable response to exit. It begs the question how decisions are arrived at that reside in *Hindsight-Latency* more firmly than *Foresight-Latency*.

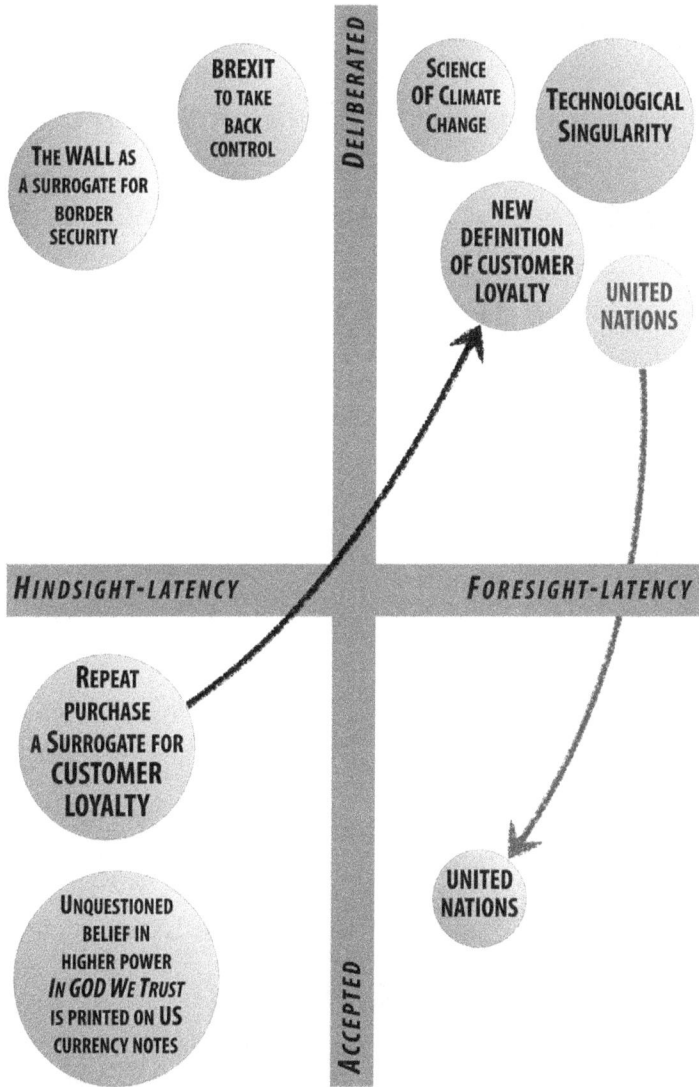

THE WALL AS A SURROGATE FOR BORDER SECURITY

BREXIT TO TAKE BACK CONTROL

SCIENCE OF CLIMATE CHANGE

TECHNOLOGICAL SINGULARITY

DELIBERATED

NEW DEFINITION OF CUSTOMER LOYALTY

UNITED NATIONS

HINDSIGHT-LATENCY

FORESIGHT-LATENCY

REPEAT PURCHASE A SURROGATE FOR CUSTOMER LOYALTY

UNQUESTIONED BELIEF IN HIGHER POWER *IN GOD WE TRUST* IS PRINTED ON US CURRENCY NOTES

ACCEPTED

UNITED NATIONS

the latency-factor map

153

In the political arena, *Hindsight-Latency* appears to display its character prominently. For instance, the interpretation of the Constitution is a contentious one. The Bill of Rights in its second amendment states: *"A well regulated Militia, being necessary to the security of a free State, the right of the people to keep and bear Arms, shall not be infringed."* Without a reasonable doubt, one can say that the founders had very cogent reasoning for the second amendment. It certainly was deliberated in the context of those times and a vision of the future that they could best comprehend based on their abilities. One of the interpretations by scholars today making the rounds is that the underlying concern while drafting the Bill of Rights was that too much power was being concentrated with the federal government since militias were often used as slave patrols at the time. Therefore, to address concerns about keeping the balance of power between federal and state, the second amendment was ratified into the Bill of Rights.

Once upon a time the Bill of Rights was barely centre stage and got very little attention from courts and scholars and so the legend goes that it was once called the lost amendment.

A clear transition for the second amendment came to fruition in quadrant [A]. The deliberations with empirical reasoning were logical and passed the test of relevance for those times.

As time went by it moved to quadrant [B] as evidenced from the fact that it was referred to as the lost amendment. This was accepted without any debate. As times changed the second amendment appears to have lost the empirical sound reasoning on which it was created. Every time there is a mass shooting and deaths are reported across

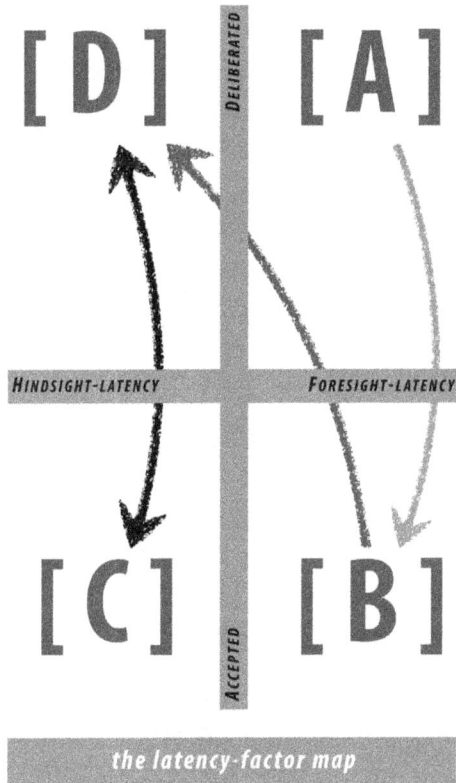

the latency-factor map

the news media the second amendment pertaining to gun rights slides into quadrant [D]. Impassioned discussions take place, albeit unsuccessfully, to get it back into quadrant [A]. Alas it slides back to quadrant [C] until such time another mass shooting occurs. The oscillation between quadrant [D] and quadrant [C] appears to be in a state of perpetual pendulum swing for many decades.

In corporate boards, various decisions are taken regularly. Some have the benefit of *Foresight-Latency* with in-depth, fact based, sound plausible assumptions upon which sales projections and revenue trends are justified and achieved. However, it is also common for *Hindsight-Latency* to silently creep in and allow decisions that lean on an assurance of past practices. Assumptions that are not challenged and drilled adequately fall prey to *Hindsight-Latency*.

In 2008 the world witnessed a phenomena that was triggered by a large decline in home prices after the collapse of a housing bubble, leading to mortgage delinquencies and foreclosures and the devaluation of housing-related securities. Everyone closely associated operated with a *Hindsight-Latency* mindset. Selling bundled securities was fine as everyone was doing it. Too big to fail was a mental shortcut that convinced everyone that nothing could go wrong. Its ramifications were worldwide. *Hindsight-Latency* phenomena prevailed.

QUESTION THE UNQUESTIONED

When a concept or an idea is constantly evaluated and challenged in a collaborative way progress in huge measure is almost certain. Immense progress in approaches in the art and science of marketing has undoubtedly served as an indicator of development. The evolution is praiseworthy as it has progressed from traditional approaches of selling and ascended to a more effective model of target marketing and now has reached a level of engagement where brands are trusted by customers. A set of shared values that invites customers to connect with, experience and be a part of.

While the discipline and practice of the art and science of marketing — in its measuring and decision making on operational parameters of customer loyalty — is not riddled with *Hindsight-Latency*, the stagnated definition of the boundaries around customer loyalty is perhaps a case of *Hindsight-Latency*. The core definition has not evolved. A clear case of adhering to strong past usage pattern and conformance to definition in citing dimensions of customer loyalty has prevailed. No wonder the murmurs about customer loyalty being dead seem to be an echo in many recent articles and reports.

Retail Dive, which is focused on providing original analysis on the latest happenings in the retail industry, reported:

> *A Forrester Research analyst at the 2015 Integrated Marketing Week made a bold statement by claiming that customer loyalty is*

dead — in part because of mobile's growth — which poses a significant problem for retailers because it is still crucial to brand success.[9a]

The idea that loyalty programs can earn and retain customer loyalty is riddled with *Hindsight-Latency*. Loyalty is a broader construct that includes trust, shared values, sacrifice and respect as evident in the words of this customer:

> *... Even if things go wrong often, I won't change my loyalty to them because I can trust that they will always work with me to make things better and that they will always care for me as a loyal customer and friend.*[9b]

Relationship and loyalty are deep-rooted and require Foresight-Latency.

IN SUMMARY — THE LATENCY FACTOR

★ Unfathomable for some as to why the definition of 'loyalty' is skewed for customers and gathers a different meaning in other walks of life. This has to do with strong patterns of adherence to usage. The stronger the usage the more distorted its meaning tends to become. The more firmly the pattern is established, the harder it becomes to break away from established notions.

★ Word meanings evolve due to pattern of usage, at times radically altering the original meaning so that words that were pure and simple get tainted with a definitive meaning that was never intended.

★ This chapter proposes the principles of the Latency Factors that appear in *Hindsight-Latency* and *Foresight-Latency*. Justifying a cause in retrospect by citing a compelling argument on reasonable grounds with plausible assumptions to open doors for progress by providing a conceptual reference (in case of *Foresight-Latency*); or shut an argument with myopic assumptions (in case of *Hindsight-Latency*).

10

What you are will show in what you do.

— *Thomas Edison*

10. THE NEW HORIZONS

there
is no
option —
we must
adapt!

I f digital is the new oil, singularity is already here. It was mind boggling to read this story in *The Economist*,[10a] "The world's most valuable resource is no longer oil, but data": *"A century ago, the resource in question was oil. Now similar concerns are being raised by the giants that deal in data, the oil of the digital era."* A thought provoking sequel[10b] continued in its editorial: "How to think about data in 2019". Reading it changed my outlook: *"Like the sticky black stuff that comes out of the ground, all those 1s and 0s are of little use until they are processed into something more valuable. That something is you."* We have been reduced to 'ones' and 'zeroes' in the digital realm, and that sticky black stuff is us — the humans.

161

On the horizon I see a wave of three macro trends — rapid progress in digital technology and AI applications, mega-trends of shifting demographics and a stark decline of trust in institutions that will create an enormous appetite for personalization and an opportunity for corporations to build relationships with their stakeholders.

THE AGE OF AI

Artificial intelligence and machine learning are raising the stakes in the analytic, predictive and executional tools race needed to develop and retain customer relationships. Simply analyzing demographic data in customer relationship management programs (CRMs) do not reveal how behavior and personal values drive buying intent. It demands more than data analytics to understand this. Advanced AI modeling helps marketers extrapolate and predict all the variables that will get a customer to engage.

Organizations like IBM, Google, Facebook, Tesla, Lenovo, Coca Cola, Adidas, Starbucks, Amazon, Netflix, Microsoft, and Uber are already using AI to grow their brands. The International Data Corporation projects that the worldwide spending on cognitive and AI systems will reach $77.6 billion in 2022. AI is being used to not just keep track of and analyze data but also to respond to queries through a chatbot and send recommendations or personalized messages. Some companies are even using voice-activated AI to interact with consumers more conversationally. Like the digital clothing marketplace Poshmark whose Alexa app called Stylist Match, uses AI to connect shoppers with the company's partner stylists. When asked, *"Alexa, ask Poshmark to style me,"* Stylist Match uses data to pair shoppers with a stylist who reflects their preferences, who in turn creates customized looks for special events like a date night, work party or casual weekend.[10c]

Companies are utilizing cognitive marketing to create targeted communications that appeal to customers individually. IBM Watson has played a pivotal role in promoting cognitive marketing and its use across various industries. As per IBM: *"Cognitive content marketing is the process of creating and distributing high-quality content to educate, engage, attract and acquire prospects into customers, customers into repeat buyers, and repeat buyers into advocates."* Refined algorithms focus on the emotional and behavioral aspects of consumer decisions and provide marketers with real-time insights that enable the personalization of online ads in order to increase their efficacy. In short, a connection is made with the customer to create loyalty and conversions.

According to Gartner, by 2020, 85% of customer interactions with the enterprise will be managed without human intervention. Powerful, innovative technology is attempting to replicate a real human touch in the relationship between a company and its customer. A dedicated account manager is no longer required to manage customer relationships. The good old bank clerk who used to update your passbook is no longer seen. Back in the day when one would call up the bank to clear a cheque the bank clerk would recognize you by your voice. Today, AI can do the same by speech recognition, natural language processing, and dialogue management.

Sophisticated neural network algorithms modeled on the human brain, and access to the explosion of data from the internet is driving deep learning. This AI technique powers self-driving cars, super-human image recognition, and life-changing — even life-saving — advances in medicine. Neuropsychopharmacology[10d] has reported that *"... deep learning has revolutionized the field of machine hearing and vision, by allowing computers to perform human-like activities including seeing, listening, and speaking."* With massive amounts of computational power, machines can now recognize objects and translate speech in real time. In the not-too-distant future, we are going to see an exponential growth in cutting-edge AI fueled software that will enhance understanding of the emotions behind consumer behaviors, and analyze and develop strategies based on that personal information to provide a personalized experience.

Already, smart AI enabled technologies are shaping the customer experience in the digital age. Brands and marketing gurus are focusing their resources on leveraging technology to optimize the customer experience to the point that it will actually encourage loyalty. While the tools to create customer loyalty are evolving at a rapid pace the very definition of 'customer loyalty' is grossly lacking and suffers from *Hindsight-Latency*. It is imperative that a new definition of 'customer loyalty' that recognizes the intrinsic facets of loyalty — willingness to sacrifice, to adjust and accommodate — is created in order to truly perfect the customer experience.

THE SHIFTING DEMOGRAPHICS

Population growth and decline in different countries, combined with an aging population, changes in ethnic mix and household size, will create a markedly different consumer market in the next three decades. By 2027, there will be six generations of consumers in the market: the *Silent Generation (1928-1945)*, *Baby Boomers (1946-1964)*, *Generation X*

(1965-1980), Millennials (1981-1997), Generation Z (1998-2016) and the *Alpha Generation (2017-?).*[10e] And one of the most significant demographic developments during this time will be Gen Z coming of age with this cohort constituting 30 percent of the world's population, including 1.5 billion adults.

Gen Z consumers are digital natives having grown up surrounded by evolving digital technologies. They are hyperconnected, yet mindful of their privacy. They are no longer defined by what they own, but by what they do. When it comes to learning about new products in the market, Gen Z places weight on the opinions of online influencers to make purchase decisions. They are spearheading a wave of change that is shaking up global consumption patterns.

Studies project Gen Z to have unparalleled buying power to the tune of $150 billion. To market to this audience and cultivate brand loyalty, brands are devising new methods that ride on the latest digital trends and seamlessly bridge the physical and digital divide. But will simply coming up with new marketing ploys be enough to capture the hearts and minds of this consumer group?

For Gen Z, their personal values influence their consumption habits more than the intrinsic value of the product or service they are consuming. Shared values confirm their loyalty to a brand, not status or prestige. They actively seek out environment friendly and socially minded brands and are willing to give them their *Share of Wallet* and pay extra for such products and services. They desire a better, cleaner and healthier world and are willing to make sacrifices to embrace brands that deliver on their social, economic and environmental responsibilities. To successfully engage with this consumer cohort, companies will have to shake off their old presumptions and assumptions and craft a new definition of 'customer loyalty' inspired by *Foresight-Latency*.

DECLINING TRUST

Hackers, spies, accounting frauds, security breaches, the Great Recession, a near constant stream of corporate scandals have imploded people's trust in institutions. Trust in corporations is eroding fast with more than 50 percent of consumers in the US, UK, France, Japan and Germany having little or no confidence in large corporations and brands. For companies trying to build and retain loyalty that is quite a steep hill to climb.

High-profile corporate privacy scandals has forced consumers to get to grips with their digital footprints and changed the way they allow themselves to trust companies — consumers are demanding that brands have clearly defined values and that those values are transparent and consistently demonstrated in everything they do and in every product or service they bring to the market.

How can brands create meaningful relationships when consumers are engulfed in doubt?

To build loyalty, trust has become an absolutely fundamental part of any brand proposition. Customers seek relationships based on trust rather than individual transactions. But how can brands earn trust? By being honest and genuine, and sticking to their values no matter what. Consumers are willing to overlook infractions and lapses, to forgive, as emphasized by the *L&S Elusive* principle if there's transparency, authenticity and an alignment of values. The *L&S Customer Loyalty* definition has the ingredients that can be applied as fundamental drivers of loyalty — what a customer is willing to forgive and forgo — as a yardstick for measuring loyalty.

I believe there is an opportunity here to engage in redefining relevant parameters in designing enterprise systems that build relationships based on *L&S Principles* and the four axioms of loyalty. Plausible ideas with a collective drive and a mindset of *Foresight-Latency* is desirable to usher progress. The choice is clear: we can either shut the door due to strong pattern of adherence to current definition of customer loyalty, or explore compelling arguments on reasonable grounds with tenable assumptions to open doors for progress. The paranoia predicting a point of no return that could change the face of human civilization has engulfed many in its vortex.

A VORTEX OF NO RETURN

It is fascinating to observe that the application of technological singularity was a concept borrowed from the black hole's 'point of no return'. It was planted into usage to shine a light on unfathomable technological disruption. This indeed is a case of *Foresight-Latency*. The technological singularity that has started a new conversation is relentlessly shaping the future world view. An ongoing deliberation on the impact of technology and impending inflection point is an undeviating march towards refining and shaping definitions and world view. Such is the power of *Foresight-Latency*. When a concept or an idea is constantly evaluated and challenged in a collaborative way progress in huge measure is almost certain.

It may be of interest and relevance to look at how technological singularity got injected into the business vocabulary. Stanislaw Ulam, a Polish-American scientist in the fields of mathematics and nuclear physics who participated in the Manhattan Project, reports a discussion (circa 1955) with John von Neumann who was responsible for injecting a borrowed concept of the point of no return from the inner ring of blackholes into technological singularity that many have cited and regarded as gospel truth. Stanislaw Ulam published a profile[10f] on John von Neumann and it states:

> *In John von Neumann's death on February 8, 1957, the world of mathematics lost a most original, penetrating, and versatile mind. Science suffered the loss of a universal intellect and a unique interpreter of mathematics, who could bring the latest (and develop latent) applications of its methods to bear on problems of physics, astronomy, biology, and the new technology.*

> *Many eminent voices have already described and praised his contributions. It is my aim to add here a brief account of his life and of his work from a background of personal acquaintance and friendship extending over a period of 25 years.*

Quite aware that the criteria of value in mathematical work are, to some extent, purely aesthetic, he once expressed an apprehension that the values put on abstract scientific achievement in our present civilization might diminish:

> *"The interests of humanity may change, the present curiosities in science may cease, and entirely different things may occupy the human mind in the future."*

Ulam continued in the profile:

> *One conversation centered on the ever accelerating progress of technology and changes in the mode of human life, which gives the appearance of approaching some essential singularity in the history of the race beyond which human affairs, as we know them, could not continue.*

A closer look reveals that the exact words about singularity is not a direct quote from John von Neumann but instead it is based on a recollection and interpretation of the conversation Stanislaw Ulam had with John von Neumann. It appears that John von Neumann was speaking metaphorically. If that were the case, then one can convincingly say, beyond a shred of doubt, that *Foresight-Latency* exists — as it is about justifying a cause in retrospect by citing a compelling argument on reasonable grounds with plausible assumptions to open doors for progress by providing a conceptual reference.

OPENING MINDS

Foresight-Latency allows comprehension of new ideas based on sound plausible assumptions that open doors for progress. Even though the simmering idea of the metaphorical concept of technological singularity was alluded to in 1955, it took 52 years for it to grace centre stage. The idea has galvanized many scholars and gurus and a constant ideation around technological singularity provides new revelations. Such is the power of *Foresight-Latency.*

Another fascinating tapestry for progress was the development of fuzzy logic. An approach to computing based on degrees of truth rather than the usual true or false (1 or 0). Resting on plausible assumptions. Paving the way for a realm of the boolean logic upon which the modern computer is based. These developments fall into the domain of *Foresight-Latency*. It has opened doors for many to contribute and advance the agenda. Advance learning and foster real progress.

In these changing times one sees two diagonally acting forces on *Foresight-Latency vs Hindsight-Latency*. While the former tends to open a collaborative vision for development and accommodating change, the latter descends into protracting a legacy definition that is confined and regimented. My way or no way is the tone and substance of the latter.

Disparate forces will always find a way to restrict and confine a desirable meaning even though from some quadrants it may appear to be a manipulative maneuver. Such is the force of *Hindsight-Latency* at play. Justifying in retrospect anything and everything that suits the current context.

The definition of customer loyalty is no exception to the rules of *Hindsight-Latency* and has been a victim of half-baked systems thinking that ignores critical parameters of loyalty factors. Opening minds to accept a new definition and explore plausible paradigms can help catapult new thinking.

There will always be resistance to new ideas no matter what. Why does lightening, despite being charged with millions of volts, not strike in a straight line but almost always follows a jagged path? Because there is always some resistance in the atmosphere. The digital age attempts to create a seamless interconnected world; yet the path is riddled with resistance. There is never a straight line even in the digital world. Legacy issues, demands of country specific laws, vulnerability from security threats — these are just a few hurdles in a long list of roadblocks.

Despite significant progress in the sphere of Internet of Things (IoT), many have facetiously called it Internet of Threats. Preventing security breaches requires a mindset of fixing glitches and revisiting definitions. Nothing can get resolved unless there is a will to evolve and amend. Make progress by refining definitions and allowing for collaborative forces to provide new ideas and new models. Everything that is backed by *Foresight-Latency* has the potential to usher in progress. With uninterrupted growth set to cause upheavals beyond the Millennials and Gen Z, the stage is set not just for new technologies but new thinking to re-define basic, worn out definitions. With a mindset of *Foresight-Latency* we are ready to galvanize innovation in technology and develop a deeper understanding about the scope of customer loyalty.

The revised definition of 'customer loyalty' in chapter 4 brings out the four axioms of loyalty that uniformly applies to employees and customers. The interconnectedness and correlation of the *L&S Principles* opens doors for measuring unknown insights that can be unearthed with the help of new technologies and refined AI approaches that are on the anvil. This indeed will require an open mind.

The empirical cause and effect between *Employee facing L&S Principles* and its direct or indirect impact on *Customer facing L&S Principles* is open to research and infusion of new insights after a foundation of ground rules are decided and laid down.

It is time to welcome ignited minds and influential, creative thinkers to engage with this subject and lead the conversation in the quadrant of *Foresight-Latency* with positive decibel levels of deliberations to help define the new systems and approaches.

What will it take to embrace the proposed broader and deeper definition of loyalty?

Can void for personalization be filled by appreciating what customers are willing to do for the brand?

What will it take to focus on not just the share of the wallet,
but recognize the appetite that loyal customers have
for accommodating and compromising
for the love of the brand
over a life cycle?

How can the new vocabulary
be part of redesigning the CRM systems
in today's digital progress?

What will it take to welcome the L&S Principles
with a Foresight-Latency and enhance its scope
with a collaborative outlook?

IN SUMMARY — THE NEW HORIZONS

★ The fascinating challenges of the new horizons and the rapid progress of the digital age with demographic and attitudinal shifts is taking human progress to new heights. The idea of technological singularity is perhaps already here.

★ The concept of *Foresight-Latency* is fascinating and applies to new developments that can open a door for empirical engagement. The dangers of getting pulled back into the *Hindsight-Latency* arguments that shut the door due to heuristics and biases, deserve to be highlighted as a caution.

★ While we recognize that the realities of new horizons need new approaches, we know that without revising the basic tenets and definitions we may not get breakthrough results. Many have amplified the limitations of the customer loyalty paradigm. We need a renewed universally potent definition of customer loyalty to usher higher progress. Here's a call to brilliant minds ready to engage with *Foresight-Latency* to take up the challenge of redefining loyalty.

The most sublime act
is to set another before you.

— *William Blake*

Acknowledgements

My late father often said to me, *"some folks can speak endlessly — as if they love to hear their own voice — but when they are asked to write down their ideas and propositions on a piece of paper they shrivel and wither away ... Son, test your mental clarity by writing out your concepts and propositions. Express your ideas in the most explicit terms first to yourself — only then will clarity emerge."* His teachings, over the years, have helped me immensely.

In my early years, like many in my generation, I was exposed to the many ideas and concepts proposed by Dr. Edward de Bono. He has inspired an entire generation and altered the trajectory of human progress with the path-breaking body of knowledge that he has created around *'thinking'*. It has been noted that Dr. de Bono is among the very few people in history who can be said to have had a significant impact on the way we think. He is equally renowned for his development of the *'Six Thinking Hats'* technique and the *'Direct Attention Thinking Tools'*. He is the originator of the concept of

'Lateral Thinking', which is now part of the English language and is listed in the Oxford English dictionary. I wish to thank Dr. Edward de Bono for reviewing my propositions and taking the time to read the entire manuscript while it was under development. An offline deliberation followed, and he wrote the Preface for this book. I wish to place on record my deep appreciation for Dr. Edward de Bono, for his engagement and his support, and all his teachings over the years. My very special thanks to Justine Cassar Gaspar — for extending her help and assiduously assisting in enabling the offline discussion with Dr. Edward de Bono for crafting the Preface.

We are a product of what we learn, how we learn, and eventually what we do with the learning. The opportunities that are given to us, challenge our thinking. Early in my career, I was fortunate to have had the chance to be ushered into the realms of the highest echelons of the corporate world where the concept of trusteeship frequently appeared in conversations. This kindled in me, an appetite for good governance. Having served clients in the B2C and B2B space while heading a creative ad agency, I decided to join the Honeywell joint venture with Tata. This was barely 50 weeks after Ratan N Tata had taken charge of the Tata conglomerate as Group Chairman. Looking back, it was just after another 50 weeks that I found myself deliberating a systems thinking proposal for the entire Tata Group. We were not satisfied with making an impact in one company. Our aspiration soared towards altering the trajectory of the entire Tata Group. This effort brought me to the corporate center and presented me an opportunity to work for Tata Sons where I had the privilege of directly working under the guidance of Ratan N Tata on numerous occasions. One of the first assignments he tasked me with was to undertake a research study on values in an organization — its nature, evolution, and need for nurturing. Propelling one's mind into uncharted territory is what great leaders do. You find yourself leading from the front in the domain of thought leadership and leaping over your mental minefields; your failures and successes are at stake. You fall, and you pick yourself up, and start all over again. Words fail me as I struggle to explain the great service Ratan Tata did to me by hurling me out into an orbit that demands nothing but excellence — for that I am truly indebted to him for life.

In my formative years, Madhu Bhagwat, who served as CEO of the Honeywell joint venture with Tata, and was a member of several boards as well as an advisor to Tata Sons, was my mentor and influenced my work life. Under his leadership, though he was head of the organization, I had the latitude to act decisively even with him. Once, during those early days, when I was racing against deadlines, I recall sending him a fax: *"Please approve by noon — if not — I will take the call and decide."* My deepest appreciation for his efforts in reading my concept note about *loyalty and sacrifice* for which I imposed no deadlines upon him.

While putting together the concept note for the book, I had loosely assembled a focus group comprising my friends and ex-colleagues. Sincerest thanks to them for listening to my ideas and willingly enduring my early drafts. During my stint in the hospitality industry I acquired a deep appreciation of the sensibilities in hospitality operations and perceived an innate desire in passionate employees to go beyond the call of duty — this awareness ignited my thinking. My many conversations with colleagues in the hospitality business made me realize that for them hospitality is not a profession. It is a way of life. Work-life balance can be possible by a self-regulated check. It cannot be forced — it is a self-imposed discipline for all passionate hoteliers. Raymond N Bickson, my former boss at Taj Hotels and a good friend, took the time to read the concept note and reaffirmed my hypothesis. David Gibbons, an exceptionally consummate hotelier and my colleague, was among the early proponents of my concepts and discussed with me the nature of my propositions. Conversations with Franz Zeller, another skilled hotelier and an ex-colleague, helped me gain insights

182

that sharpened my understanding about the tenets of service. Birgit Zorniger, a refined hospitality consultant with an eye for detail and years of experience across three continents, took the time to read the raw form of my manuscript.

With his diverse experience in hospitality and Fast-Moving Consumer Goods, Kasi Srinivasan, my colleague and friend, encouraged me and served as my sounding board. The astute Uday Narain, with a background in business development and leading businesses in real estate and hospitality, invested time to study my initial drafts. I must thank Mani Venkataraman, an accomplished consulting professional, and now heading a digital business among the big four, for his helpful insights. Special thanks to Jaisinh Dhembre — a dynamic, seasoned IT executive director working in one of the top four consulting firms with experience that cuts across multiple industries and countries across the globe — who was most generous with his time for engaging in discussions. My special thanks to Kaikhushru 'Kai' Taraporevala who serves as a Non-Executive Director and senior corporate finance advisor with extensive experience across the ASEAN and Indian subcontinents, for his valuable inputs.

Nothing worthwhile can ever be published without diligent editorial support. I had the benefit of working with the finest editorial minds who have criticized my narrative as the manuscript took shape and evolved. Ajay Kumar — a former executive editor of a national newspaper, an avid reader who has held his own, and my friend and colleague — was extremely helpful in shaping the narrative flow. He took out the time to read the manuscript several times and offer his feedback. I have had the pleasure of working with him on several assignments while he served as VP – Communications in the office of Ratan N Tata, and together we have burnt the midnight oil countless times, while meeting deadlines. During our association over the years, I have benefited immensely from his editorial mind. A big thanks to him.

As work on the manuscript started to pick up momentum and it was time to flesh out my ideas, I happened to reconnect with my ex-colleague and friend Banshi Talukdar. She expressed a desire to work together again on something inspiring and insightful. Despite our travels as we hopped across three countries over the past four months, the manuscript was written and edited. Thanks to online collaboration. This age of technological advancement is truly a blessing. Her precise comprehension of the scope of research required for this book, clarity of expression, and her thorough editorial skills with a good eye for detail, is by far *par excellence*. I could not have delivered on this project without her timely help and support. I must also thank Radhika Panjwani for providing a fresh perspective with her feedback.

Life brings awareness of itself when the email is signed off with: *"Happy to be alive!"* I have enjoyed knowing this brilliant and seasoned executive, Max Henry, who is leveraging his vast experience to offer mentorship to start-ups. I understand Steve Jobs used to remark *"... Max's special DNA as applied to engendering the loyalty and results of high performing teams."* Yes, Max worked with one of the most admired leaders of this century. Max's keen senses to spot and appreciate new ideas is indeed an asset. He painstakingly read the manuscript and voiced his *Do's* and *Don'ts*, besides bringing in Maxwell Sims as an additional focus group member. Maxwell's enthusiasm was infectious and his background in cognitive neuroscience made him a valuable sounding board.

Over the years, there have been many who shared their experiences and influenced my thinking and willingly collaborated — for that I am eternally grateful.

Raghu Kalé

In the long history of humankind
(and animal kind, too) those who learned to collaborate
and improvise most effectively have prevailed.

— *Charles Darwin*

List of References

The list of references is provided in the sequence they appear in the book.

1a   Kashmir Hill, "How Target Figured Out A Teen Girl Was Pregnant Before Her Father Did," *Forbes*, Feb 16, 2012: *https://www.forbes.com/sites/kashmirhill/2012/02/16/how-target-figured-out-a-teen-girl-was-pregnant-before-her-father-did/#917ee7d66686.*

1b   Andrew Keen, "How the Internet Is Threatening Our Freedom," *Politico*, May 18, 2016: *https://www.politico.com/magazine/story/2016/05/2016-election-internet-campaign-facts-digital-new-media-213899.*

1c   Issie Lapowsky, "How Cambridge Analytica Sparked the Great Privacy Awakening," *Wired*, Mar17, 2019: *https://www.wired.com/story/cambridge-analytica-facebook-privacy-awakening/.*

1d   Vanessa Friedman and Jonah Engel Bromwich, "Cambridge Analytica Used Fashion Tastes to Identify Right-Wing Voters," *The New York Times*, Nov 29, 2018: *https://www.nytimes.com/2018/11/29/style/cambridge-analytica-fashion-data.html.*

1e   Sheera Frenkel, Nicholas Confessore, Cecilia Kang, Matthew Rosenberg and Jack Nicas, "Delay, Deny and Deflect: How Facebook's Leaders Fought Through Crisis," *The New York Times*, Nov 14, 2018:
https://www.nytimes.com/2018/11/14/technology/facebook-data-russia-election-racism.html.

2a   O. Henry, *The Gift of the Magi and Other Short Stories.*

2b   *Financial Times* Lexicon:
http://lexicon.ft.com/Term?term=customer-loyalty.

2c   *Online Etymology Dictionary*:
https://www.etymonline.com/word/loyalty.

3a   Akshaya Kumar Sahoo, "Brave Doberman Kills 4 Cobras to Save Eight of Master's Family, Dies," *The Deccan Chronicle*, Jul 14, 2016:
https://www.deccanchronicle.com/nation/in-other-news/140716/brave-doberman-kills-4-cobras-to-save-eight-of-masters-family-dies.html.

3b   Hal Conick, "What Businesses can Learn from the Military," Nov 30, 2015:
https://www.kellogg.northwestern.edu/news_articles/2015/11302015-kellogg-growth-forum-mcmaster.aspx.

3c   Bill Murphy Jr., "23 Things Great Leaders Always Do," *inc.com*, Jun 13, 2014:
https://www.inc.com/bill-murphy-jr/23-things-great-leaders-always-do.html.

3d   Adapted from Harinder Sikka, *Calling Sehmat* (India: Penguin Random House, 2018).

3e   Rohit Deshpande, Terror at the Taj Bombay: Customer-Centric Leadership, Harvard Business School Multimedia/Video Case 511-703, Mar 2011.

3f   Rakesh Krishnan Simha, "The Men who Starved to Death to Save the World's Seeds," *Russia Beyond*, May 12, 2014: *https://www.rbth.com/blogs/2014/05/12/ the_men_who_starved_to_death_to_save_the_worlds_seeds_35135.*

3g   David M. Thomas, "One Lieutenant's Ultimate Gift to America," *The Washington Post*, Dec 25, 2017: *https://www.washingtonpost.com/opinions/one-lieutenants-ultimate-gift-to- america/2017/12/25/55c1fff0-e69b-11e7- ab50-621fe0588340_story.html?noredirect=on&utm_term=.ddf252da4838.*

4a   "Customer Loyalty Myths Debunked," *Gartner*: *https://www.gartner.com/en/sales-service/insights/effortless-experience/ customer-loyalty-myths.*

4b   Augie Ray, "The Customer Experience Difference: Are Customers Loyal to Your Brand or Your Loyalty Program?," *Gartner for Marketers* (blog), Nov 20, 2018: *https://blogs.gartner.com/augie-ray/2018/11/20/the-customer-experience- difference-are-customers-loyal-to-your-brand-or-your-loyalty-program/.*

4c   Nicole Leinbach-Reyhle, "Customer Loyalty in Today's Modern Retail World," *Forbes*, Apr 20, 2016: *https://www.forbes.com/sites/nicoleleinbachreyhle/2016/04/20/customer- loyalty-in-todays-modern-retail-world/#76188a29513c.*

5a   Christina Zdanowicz, "Recalls don't Scare some Loyal Toyota
      Fans," *CNN*, Feb 4, 2010:
      http://edition.cnn.com/2010/US/02/04/toyota.loyal.irpt/index.html.

5b   Alice Gomstyn, "Toyota Recalls More Cars, But Customers Stay
      Loyal," *ABC News*, Feb 9, 2010:
      https://abcnews.go.com/Business/toyota-customers-defend-brand-recalls/story?
      id=9781832.

5c   Ezra Dyer, "I Envy the Blind Faith of the Brand-Loyal Car
      Shopper," *Car And Driver*, Mar 17, 2016:
      https://www.caranddriver.com/features/a15102391/i-envy-the-blind-faith-
      of-the-brand-loyal-car-shopper-column/.

5d   T. John, "Are Harley-Davidsons the Best Motorcycles?," May 11,
      2018:
      https://www.quora.com/Are-Harley-Davidsons-the-best-motorcycles.

5e   Michel Hogan, "We're all Human: Why Customers Need to be
      More Forgiving," *SmartCompany*, Apr 2, 2019:
      https://www.smartcompany.com.au/marketing/public-relations/customers-
      more-forgiving/.

5f   2018 Temkin Forgiveness Ratings, Apr 24, 2018:
      https://experiencematters.blog/2018/04/24/2018-temkin-forgiveness-
      ratings/.

5g   Jeff Joireman, Yany Grégoire and Thomas M Tripp, "Customer
      Forgiveness following Service Failures," *Current Opinion in Psychology*
      10, (2016): 76-82:
      https://doi.org/10.1016/j.copsyc.2015.11.005.

6a   James D. Roumeliotis, "Identifying and Catering to the Discerning Consumer: Quality and Service Above All," Sep 24, 2015: *https://www.linkedin.com/pulse/identifying-catering-discerning-consumer-quality-all-roumeliotis.*

6b   Hazel Plush, "The Most Ridiculous Requests made by Travellers on Private Jets," *The Telegraph*, Sep 1, 2016: https://www.telegraph.co.uk/travel/lists/outrageous-requests-people-make-when-travelling-by-private-jet/.

6c   Ben Feldheim, "The Wildest Things I've Witnessed Working as a Stewardess on Private Jets," *Mel Magazine: https://melmagazine.com/en-us/story/the-wildest-things-ive-witnessed-working-as-a-stewardess-on-private-jets.*

6d   Zachary Weiss, "From Divorce Papers to Dog Food: The Most Ridiculous Private Jet Requests," *Observer*, Aug 9, 2016: *https://observer.com/2016/08/from-divorce-papers-to-dog-food-the-most-over-the-top-private-jet-requests/.*

6e   Marie, "It's Harley Time — But Is It Worth the Cost?," *Prairie Eco-Thrifter*, Apr 6, 2012, Retrieved from "Would you risk your home to own a motorcycle?" *https://prairieecothrifter.com/2012/04/harley-time-worth-cost.html.*

6f   Erika Adams, "Hermès Birkin Owners Reveal Crazy Tips for Buying the Bag," *Vox*, Jun 26, 2015: *https://www.vox.com/2015/6/26/8850883/hermes-birkin-bags.*

7a   "Meet the Starbucks Barista Who is Learning Sign Language for a Customer," *Starbucks Stories*, Feb 26, 2016: *https://news.starbucks.com/news/starbucks-barista-learns-sign-language-for-a-customer.*

7b   Barbara Apple Sullivan, "The True Story of Amazing Customer Service from —Gasp! — An Airline," *Fast Company*, Jun 14, 2013: *https://www.fastcompany.com/3012939/the-true-story-of-amazing-customer-service-from-gasp-an-airline.*

7c   Marie Rosecrans, "Everything I Need to Know About Customer Service, I Learned at Nordstrom," *Salesforce* (blog), May 8, 2014: *https://www.salesforce.com/blog/2014/05/nordstrom-customer-service.html.*

7d   Telus, "Above and Beyond: 5 True Stories of Exceptional Customer Service," *Times Colonist*, Jan 22, 2016: *https://www.timescolonist.com/life/above-and-beyond-5-true-stories-of-exceptional-customer-service-1.2156788.*

7e   Stan Phelps, "Heroic Customer Service by a Senior Executive at Warby Parker," *Forbes*, Aug 1, 2014: *https://www.forbes.com/sites/stanphelps/2014/08/01/heroic-customer-service-by-a-senior-executive-at-warby-parker/#23f18c714c9f.*

7f   N. Avon, "Pilot holds Flight for Man going to see Dying Grandson," *CNN*, Jan 14, 2011, Retrieved from: *http://edition.cnn.com/2011/TRAVEL/01/14/southwest.pilot.holds.flight/index.html.*

7g   Minnie Gupta, Boston, Jan 2018.

7h Aliyah Frumin, "Airline Employee goes Above and Beyond to Return Bag to 'Panicking' Cancer Patient," *Today*, Aug 9, 2017, *https://www.today.com/health/airline-employee-goes-above-beyond-return-bag-panicking-cancer-patient-t114914*.

7i "Amazingly SHOCKING Customer Experience Stories: Nordstrom sets a Shiny Example!," *Customer Guru* (blog): *https://www.customerguru.in/amazingly-shocking-customer-experience-stories-nordstrom-sets-a-shiny-example/*.

7j Dominique Mosbergen, "How Ordering Domino's Pizza Daily Saved a Man's Life," *HuffPost*, Nov 5, 2016: *https://www.huffingtonpost.in/entry/dominos-pizza-saves-mans-life_us_5732a349e4b096e9f0932e0c?ec_carp=1907099482263698032*.

8a Cindy Sui, "Taking on the Family Firm: A Daughter's Reluctant Journey," *BBC*, Nov 10, 2015: *https://www.bbc.com/news/business-34773694*.

8b Fritz Schumann, Houshi: *https://vimeo.com/114879061*.

8c Jordana Rothman, "What Does It Mean To Be Born Into a Legendary Restaurant Family?," *MAD*, Apr 8, 2015: *https://www.madfeed.co/2015/what-does-it-mean-to-be-born-into-a-legendary-restaurant-family/*.

8d Jordana Rothman, "What Does It Mean To Be Born Into a Legendary Restaurant Family?," *MAD*, Apr 8, 2015: *https://www.madfeed.co/2015/what-does-it-mean-to-be-born-into-a-legendary-restaurant-family/*.

9a   Brielle Jaekel, "Forrester Analyst: Customer Loyalty is Dead but still Vital for Retailers," *Retail Dive*: *https://www.retaildive.com/ex/mobilecommercedaily/forrester-analyst-customer-loyalty-is-dead-but-still-vital-for-retailers.*

9b   Adrian Swinscoe, "Loyalty Is Dead, Long Live Loyalty!," *Forbes*, Oct 14, 2018: *https://www.forbes.com/sites/adrianswinscoe/2018/10/14/loyalty-is-dead-long-live-loyalty/#41c379676adf.*

10a   "The World's Most Valuable Resource is no Longer Oil, but Data," *The Economist*, May 6, 2017: *https://www.economist.com/leaders/2017/05/06/the-worlds-most-valuable-resource-is-no-longer-oil-but-data.*

10b   "How to Think about Data in 2019," *The Economist*, Dec 22, 2018: *https://www.economist.com/leaders/2018/12/22/how-to-think-about-data-in-2019.*

10c   Julia Stead, "How AI Can Inspire Consumers and Build Stronger Brand Loyalty," *Adweek*, Sep 19, 2018: *https://www.adweek.com/digital/how-ai-can-inspire-consumers-and-build-stronger-brand-loyalty/.*

10d   Kevin R. Coffey, Russell G. Marx and John F. Neumaier, "DeepSqueak: A Deep Learning-based System for Detection and Analysis of Ultrasonic Vocalizations," *Neuropsychopharmacology* 44, (2019): 859–868: *https://www.nature.com/articles/s41386-018-0303-6.*

10e   Mirko Warschun, Imran Dassu and Natalie Shield, "The Consumers of the Future: Influence vs. Affluence," *A. T. Kearney Global Future Consumer Study*, 2017: *https://www.atkearney.com/documents/20152/815769/2017+The+Consumers+of+the+Future-+Influence+vs.+Affluence.pdf/6efbcc9a-2b1c-8269-daf8-593e47155886*

10f   Stanislaw Ulam, *Bulletin of the American Mathematical Society*, 64 (1958), 1-49: *https://doi.org/10.1090/S0002-9904-1958-10189-5.*

Be who you are and say what you feel,
because those who mind don't matter,
and those who matter don't mind.

— Bernard Baruch

Author Introduction by Raymond N Bickson

orking with Raghu for over a decade was a distinct pleasure — at the time I was the CEO of Taj Hotels Resorts and Palaces and served on many boards in the hospitality vertical of the Tata conglomerate. I have had the pleasure of calling him both a colleague and a trusted friend. For some, the power of conceptual thinking comes naturally; Raghu demonstrated an intuitive sense of the bigger picture, as well as the ability to translate abstract thoughts, proactively thinking in longterm horizons and the desire to experiment and invent new things.

Reading the manuscript I realized it is aptly crafted for leaders, practitioners and academic thinkers to further the conversation on this very pertinent subject.

In my personal experience of dealing with guests in hospitality, instances of passionate associates who go beyond the call of duty is always inspiring.

We readily acknowledge the sacrifice embedded in the loyalty displayed by soldiers. We are also humbled by the loyalty displayed by company colleagues like the employees of the Taj Hotel in Mumbai in 2008 when many of them sacrificed their lives to protect the hotel's guests from terrorists.

Our close encounter with crisis during the terror attacks in 2008 serves as a painful memory. The wrath of nature in 2005 in the Tsunami that ravaged coastal humanity across the Indian Ocean was agonizing. These experiences are a source for reflection. These are life changing events and the uplifting deeds of countless souls during these harrowing times affected us deeply. Throughout our lives we witness and encounter events — some small, some colossal — that enlighten us and elevate our senses. Raghu has connected the dots in proposing the interplay between loyalty and sacrifice.

The main proposition in this book is that we fail to acknowledge the sacrifice inherent in the loyalty displayed by customers towards their favored brands. This key strategic oversight, Raghu argues, has come about because of the limitations of the human mind.

Sacrifice is inseparable from loyalty and that begs the question — *are customers capable of sacrifice?* Indeed a uniform definition of the term 'loyalty' as applied to employees and customers and any stakeholder, will pave the way for a new paradigm. Unearth hidden possibilities, and for this, a new vantage point is needed which has been proposed in this book. What makes this book relevant is that the developments in artificial intelligence, robotics, bio-metrics and Big Data hold the promise for significant advancement in understanding the human mind.

This truism is the perspective which informs this exploration into the relationship between loyalty and sacrifice as succinctly brought out by Raghu Kalé.

For those who saw him from a distance, Raghu's strategic and conceptual powers were overshadowed by his wizardry in film making and creative pursuits. His involvement enhanced the effectiveness and impact of many communication initiatives that we collaborated on; his strategic insights enabling the translation of business realities to strengthen the fabric of communication during my stewardship at Taj Hotels for over a decade.

Raghu was always much more than a communicator. He was among the pioneers engaged in proposing a systems view to strengthen organizational performance excellence. He played a crucial role in proposing (and later) implementing an organizational assessment initiative, culminating into an award that was fashioned on the lines of the Baldrige excellence criteria of USA. It eventually became the Tata Business Model of Excellence — a holistic framework for Tata companies to be on a continuous journey of improving their competitiveness.

The Tata Business Model assessment required companies to be perpetually restless in examining the clarity and validity of their strategy. The Chairman of the Tata Group, Ratan N Tata would often exhort: *"question the unquestionable"*, and it is pleasing to note that Raghu has done precisely that. Raghu draws on his deep understanding of business strategy to question some of the known beliefs around customer loyalty.

This slim treatise is not a business manual, crammed with answers to the challenges identified by it. This is a conceptual book which asks the right questions to try and expand our knowledge frontiers on the key strategic aspect of customer loyalty.

This book is an invitation to experts in related fields to improve our existing metrics for measuring human behavior through the use of futuristic technologies. This will need revisiting of old and obsolete definitions and the fashioning of new approaches to understand the complexities of the human mind.

It is my hope that the book will ignite a new conversation that will impart momentum to human progress.

Raymond N Bickson
PRINCIPAL & CEO, BICKSON HOSPITALITY GROUP LLC

Author's Profile

Raghu Kalé is an accomplished communications professional who has positively impacted business outcomes by supporting corporate and operational strategy.

He has worked with corporate board members and business leaders, helping alter the conversations for leadership with his creative, divergent thinking.

His systems thinking approach in leading communication has helped reconfigure efficiency and productivity by developing a trans-disciplinary understanding of the realities about running and changing a business and making sustainable impacts to deliver performance — while being mindful of the scalability for developing future organizational capabilities.

In his experience spanning over two and a half decades he has worked in technology companies, corporate services, consulting, hospitality and advertising.

His divergent thinking brings out stunning and striking ideas rooted in experiences that find an expression in myriad, result-oriented business initiatives — in thought provoking articles, original concepts, creative films, and books. His ability to connect with people on an honest level helps him draw out their deepest insights and opinions — a trait which he has leveraged to build compelling stories in the form of short documentary films. His other interests include photography and music.

Formerly, Raghu was Vice President — Office of the Brand Custodian, Tata Sons, and supported brand and marketing thought leadership initiatives. Currently, he is the CEO of Striking Ideas LLC and working on his next book *The Latency Factor*.

Raghu lives in New Jersey with his wife Ywin Shin, their daughters, and their beagle named Skyé.